How to be Your Own Best Editor

How to be Your Own Best Editor

An essential toolkit for everyone who writes.

Barry Tarshis

 iUniverse®

HOW TO BE YOUR OWN BEST EDITOR
AN ESSENTIAL TOOLKIT FOR EVERYONE WHO WRITES.

iUniverse books may be ordered through booksellers or by contacting:

iUniverse
1663 Liberty Drive
Bloomington, IN 47403
www.iuniverse.com
844-349-9409

ISBN: 978-1-5320-6890-4 (sc)
ISBN: 978-1-5320-6891-1 (e)

Print information available on the last page.

iUniverse rev. date: 06/24/2021

Contents

1

Get into the Right Mind Set

L et's not pussyfoot. The biggest obstacle you have to overcome when you edit your own writing is you, which is to say everything you have already come to know and feel about a document that you yourself have produced and that you yourself must now scrutinize and administer to. How do you get around the fact, for example, that having written them yourself, you already know what the words are *supposed* to mean? And how do you neutralize whatever emotional attachments may have already taken hold between you and the sentences and paragraphs that are still moist from the blood, sweat, and tears you have poured into them?

The simple answer to both of these questions is that there are no answers—no practical answers, at any rate. For until you can figure out a way to rewire your nervous system, I don't care how much time you've spent counting your breaths at a Zen monastery: Viewing your own work with absolute objectivity is a mental Everest whose summit you will never reach.

What's the alternative? Simply this: to accept the fact that self-bias is an occupational hazard of self-editing, and to adopt a mental approach and a set of practices that will help to keep this hazard reasonably at bay. Here are five suggestions whose purpose is to give you a leg up on a problem you'll never entirely solve.

1. **Create a time barrier.** It is always wise to let any document you've written and are about to edit "sit" for a spell before you start to red-pencil your way through it. An ideal sitting period would be, oh, five or six years. Otherwise, fifteen minutes will suffice—just as long as you use that fifteen minutes to clear your mind. Sort your laundry. Organize your desk. Watch *Oprah*. Buy the Houston Astros. Do anything that doesn't relate to writing—and doesn't eat into any of the mental energy you're going to be needing later on.

2. **Change the "look" of the document.** Gay Talese, the former *New York Times* reporter and *Esquire* contributing editor who has written several best-selling nonfiction books, once told me that *his* way of gaining perspective on his own work is to tack manuscript pages to a wall in his office, and then to peer at each page from the other side of the room through a pair of binoculars.

   Talese's ritual may seem bizarre to you, but don't be too quick to dismiss its utility. Neuroscientists have recently discovered that regardless of how old-sock familiar a stimulus may be, the tiniest of variations can "trick" your brain (momentarily, at least) into thinking that it is processing a stimulus it has never encountered before. The practical implication to self-editing: You're more alert.

   Virtually any visual change can make a difference. If you use a computer when you write and revise, for example, try to do your editing on hard copy, leaving plenty of space between the lines and in the margins so that you can make notes and record your changes. Don't ask me why (maybe it has something to do with the angle of your head), but if you are like most people, you can focus more attentively on words and sentences that are looking *up* at you from a sheet of paper, as opposed to looking *out* at you from a computer screen.

True, if you use a computer to write, editing on hard copy means that you or your computer slave must eventually input the changes. But the trade-off here—extra time and labor for better quality writing—is not what I would call a pact with the devil. And while I'm on the subject of visual change, think about doing your hard-copy editing at a location other than your usual writing place—and for the same general reason: to prevent your brain from being lulled into a state of "been-there-done-that" complacency.

If you have no choice other than to edit on screen (you're on an airplane whose business-class accoutrements do not include a laser printer), try changing the way the words actually appear on the screen. Bump up the size, or change the style of the font. Convert everything to boldface, or expand the space between the lines. If you have a color monitor, switch the color of the screen characters. I often play with color when I write or edit, using different colors to tell me how "finished" a particular section of the writing is. Among other things, color-coding the text helps me establish priorities: I can scroll through the document and see at a glance which sections need the most work.

3. **Read the writing out loud.** *Listening* to your writing as you read it aloud will often alert you to shortcomings that could slip by if you were reading the document silently. The trick is to read slowly and to pay attention to how the writing *flows*. If I find myself stumbling (or running out of breath) while I am reading one of my sentences aloud, it's a safe bet the sentence needs work. I've heard of some writers who go so far as to record their writing into a tape recorder, and then, with the manuscript or computer screen in front of them, play back the recording and note which sections are still rough around the edges.

An even better option, if you can manage it (and if the importance of the document warrants it), is to recruit somebody to read your writing aloud to you. This option assumes, of course, that the document is not as lengthy as *War and Peace*, and that the person you recruit is disciplined enough to suppress cruel giggles. Generally speaking, though, you would be amazed at how much attention you pay to your own writing when somebody else is reading it aloud.

4. **Don't force the issue.** As I will be emphasizing in the next chapter, it isn't until you've had a chance read through a document from start to finish that you can get a rough fix on how many problems you will eventually need to address in your editing, or how difficult it's going to be to solve those problems. The one thing you can pretty much bet the farm on, though, is that some problems you stumble across will take you less time and less effort to solve than others. And what you don't want to do, if you can possibly avoid it, is to get so bogged down trying to solve one or two unusually nasty problems that you don't have any time or energy left to address all the other problems that need to be addressed.

A good way to avoid this common editing pitfall (and to enhance your editing efficiency in the process) is to do your editing in "sweeps." Here's what I mean: Instead of trying to complete all your edits during one start-to-finish march through the document, be prepared to go through the document several times, tackling the easier-to-solve problems during the early "sweeps" and setting aside the more resistant problems until the later sweeps.

The tricky part about executing this strategy is deciding how much time and effort you should be spending on a problem before you decide to let it pass until the next sweep. My advice is to push but not press. In other words, do what you can reasonably do to fix the problem, but don't keep banging your head against a wall that isn't budging. As long as there are other solvable problems in the document that warrant your attention, keep moving ahead.

Eventually, alas, you will run out of "easy" problems and will have to go *mano a mano* with the problems you've been avoiding in the earlier sweeps. But what often happens to me when I follow this practice is this: Problems that might have taken me several minutes to solve during the first or second sweep (if indeed I solved them) become a lot easier to solve in subsequent sweeps, when I'm more focused on *that* problem.Well, sometimes. Other times I have no choice other than to slug it out with a particular problem and to settle with the best solution I can come up with.

5. **Keep a sharp mental edge.** Editing is tough, exacting work—the mental equivalent of pumping iron. To do it even reasonably well, you need a clear head and a deep reservoir of mental energy.

   In light of these demands, it is never in your best interests to edit when you are physically or mentally fatigued, when you're preoccupied with other priorities in your life, or when you're pressed for time—running late, say, for your four-year-old's first dance recital. What invariably happens in these situations is that your brain either shuts down or races ahead, and, in either case, prevents you from achieving the laser-like concentration that you need in order to get the most out of your editing efforts.

   One last piece of advice: Regardless of how clear-headed or energetic you are, or how much time you can afford to spend on your editing, try to do your editing in relatively short, highly focused segments—no more than twenty or twenty-five minutes at a time—punctuated by brief breaks. And if at any time during these segments you catch your mind drifting—you're looking at the words but you're thinking about global warming, your upcoming dentist appointment, or the last-second touchdown that cost your favorite football team a victory the day before—put the document on ice for a couple of moments, and do whatever you have to do (stretch, take deep breaths, splash cold water on your face, or swig more coffee) to get your mind back to where it belongs. Sharp pencils are a good thing to have when you edit. A sharp mind is better.

2

Set Priorities

Word has it that Oscar Wilde, the nineteenth-century Irish playwright and poet, was so fussy about his writing that he would sometimes ruminate for as many as five or six hours over a single comma decision. Without knowing which specific comma decisions prompted these ruminations, who's to say whether the results justified the effor. But it's probably a moot point. The importance of precise comma placement notwithstanding, not too many of us are in a position to emulate Wilde's work habits. Oscar Wilde, remember, did at least some of his writing during the two years he spent in Reading Gaol, a British prison. And even when he wasn't behind bars, he never had to factor into his comma-related ruminations the 6:00 p.m. pickup deadline of Federal Express, or snippy voice-mail messages from antsy clients, or impatient publishers.

No need to belabor the point. Unless the biggest problem in your life right now is that ever since you cashed out of Microsoft, you have far more time on your hands than you know what to do with, you do not have much choice. One way or another, you need to incorporate the time factor in your editing decisions. This means, for starters, that you need to set reasonable limits on how much time you spend, overall, editing any particular document. But more important—and more difficult to pull off—you need to set limits

7

on how much time you allocate to each of the individual problems you run into *within* the document.

Do not underestimate the difficulty of putting into practice either of these principles, particularly the second one. As I stressed in the Introduction, most of the decisions you need to make as an editor are subjective—a matter of taste and judgment. This means that, strictly speaking, there are no inherent or finite limits on either the number of passages in any given document that could conceivably benefit from judicious editing, and no inherent or finite limit, either, on the time and effort you ought to be spending on each passage. To complicate an already complicated scenario, the squeakiest wheel in a creaky document doesn't automatically warrant the most grease. It depends, figuratively speaking, on how big a wheel it really is, relative to all the other squeaky wheels.

Mundane though these issues may seem, you disregard them at your own peril, and at the peril, too, of the documents you edit. For if you fail to manage your time properly when you edit, you are likely to fall victim to what might best be described as the "careful-start, sloppy-finish" syndrome.

The script goes like this: You attack the early pages or early sections of a document with the intensity of an over-zealous customs agent. Gradually, however, it begins to dawn on you that in light of the deadline you're up against, you are not going to be able to linger as long on the problems that lie *ahead* of you in the document as you lingered on the problems you've already worked on and solved. So you accelerate the pace, and, guess what, you lose the critical edge. Which could explain, by the way, why the quality of so many articles and books you read, or movies you see, tends to diminish the further into the work you get. Some people attribute this phenomenon to careless workmanship. It could just as well be careless time management.

DECIDING WHAT'S IMPORTANT

It's one thing to recognize how important it is to manage your time wisely when you edit, but something else again to determine which priorities ought to be driving your time-allocation decisions. The pesky fly in this ointment is that it is risky—make that, impossible—to generalize. Normally, for instance, you would never dream of ruminating for five or six hours over where best to insert a comma. But if the comma decision involved, say, a slogan destined to be the centerpiece of a $500 million advertising campaign, not only might you want to ruminate for that length of time, you might also want to recruit a cadre of comma experts.

The best advice I can offer you by way of helping you work out a sensible, real-world time-management strategy for editing is to adopt what my friend Warren Picower calls the "big-stuff-first" approach to editing. Picower, who has been a senior-level editor for several national publications, including *Food and Wine* and *Money,* shares with most savvy editors the following philosophy: that you keep your red pencil holstered until you've had a chance to read through the entire document at least once or, better still, two or three times.

The rationale is this: Before you start to cut down, trim, or transplant any of the "trees" in a document, you want to get as clear a picture as possible of what the "forest" looks like. The main thing to avoid, Picower cautions, is wearing down the point of your red pencil on sentences and paragraphs in which the content either needs to be overhauled, or doesn't belong in the document in the first place.

Then again, you may have your own perverse reasons for fussing over sentences that, by all rights, ought to be in Sentence Heaven by the time a document is ready for editing. Your idea of a "fun evening" might be to get out the old ironing board and spend several hours ironing shirts or blouses you never intend to wear.

Assuming, though, that you manifest no such neuroses, I would urge you to organize your editing time according to the priorities I am about to spell out for you. This sequence of priorities represents the collective wisdom of a half-dozen or so of the professional book and magazine editors I've worked with over the years, and it is as applicable to editing your own work as it is to editing in general. Here they are:

> ➤ Objective
> ➤ Content
> ➤ Line-by-line editing
> ➤ Proofreading

REVISITING THE OBJECTIVE

The most productive first step to take when you start to edit your own work is to re-ask yourself the question you should have asked yourself when you first began to think about the document you're now editing, and the same question that should have been reverberating in your brain throughout the entire process. The question is this: What is the purpose of this document?

I know what some of you are thinking. Why go *backwards*? Why dwell, as an editor, on a question that you should have already addressed and resolved as a writer?

Point well taken—except for a couple of not-so-minor considerations.

First of all, more writers than you might imagine never get around to asking themselves this simple but critical question at *any* point in the process. They're too busy worrying about what they want to *say*, and how to say it. You may be one such writer.

Second, even if you took the time early on in the process to formulate an objective, it doesn't hurt to revisit that objective before you start to dig into the wording and structure of individual sentences and paragraphs. One of the occupational hazards of writing is getting so caught in the trench warfare of word choice and sentence construction that you lose sight of why you are writing in the first place—and who's going to be reading what you've written. If you don't believe me, ask yourself why editing exists as a profession unto itself. It's because writers, children that we are, can't always be trusted to produce documents that are appropriately targeted— that is, organized, slanted, and written to satisfy the requirements of a specific situation, or the needs and expectations of a specific audience.

Happily, I can recommend a simple tool that could make this whole business of clarifying your objective a good deal easier to manage than you might think. I call it the Outcome Statement.

The Outcome Statement: a closer look

An Outcome Statement is nothing more than a sentence or two that spells out what you want the document you have been writing and are now editing to *accomplish*, quite apart from what it says, or how it says it. What response, in other words, do you want to elicit from your readers? What would you like them to know, think, feel, or actually do after having read the document.

You needn't worry too much about how you actually word the Outcome Statement. And the statement doesn't have to actually appear in the document. Its purpose is purely strategic. It sets a target, as you will see when you read the Outcome Statement that has fueled the writing and editing decisions I've made in connection with this book:

> *I want the readers of this book to be able to operate more effectively as editors of their own work, and I want them to feel excited about the prospect of putting into practice the ideas and tools they learn from this book.*

What's worth noting about this Outcome Statement is its specificity. It does more than simply describe what this book is about. It spells out what the book needs to *do* if it is to accomplish the outcome I have envisioned. As such, this outcome has compelled me throughout this book to do more than simply present information clearly and concisely, but also to present it as interestingly and engagingly as I could.

A well-thought-out Outcome Statement does this for you: In addition to setting up a target for you, it helps you figure out what you need to do to hit the bull's-eye.

Statements that might be applied to specific situations. Each of them completes the following statement: *As a result of reading this document, I want my reader(s) to...*

> BUSINESS SITUATION
> *...recognize why our company is superior to our wretched and evil competitors, and be strongly motivated to award us this contract.*

> CELEBRITY PROFILE FOR MAGAZINE
> *...understand and appreciate why Daffy Duck is one of the most underrated web-footed actors in American film (and a more serious artist than Donald Duck).*

> INVESTOR NEWSLETTER
> *...be aware of—but not be hysterical about—the risks of investing in pork-belly futures.*

To add more utility to this tool, I recommend that you write the statement out on a five-by-eight index card—and IN LARGE PRINT—and that you post it in a highly visible place: on the side of your computer screen, next to your coffee mug, or—who knows, beside your eight-by-ten portrait of Oscar Wilde. That way, the target you're aiming at will never be out of your sight for more than a few seconds.

QUALITY-CHECK THE CONTENT

Here's a humbling thought for writers (nonfiction writers, in particular) who take great pride in their writing *style*: With rare exceptions, readers are far more interested in the *content* of the document than they are in the style of the writing. So the *writing* but also on the quality, the accuracy, and the relevance of the content.

You could argue once again that we're backtracking, dwelling on issues that should have been addressed and resolved earlier in the process. I'm compelled to remind you yet again, though, of how easy it is to get so caught up in the "writing" that you lose sight of *why* you're writing and who is going to be reading what you've written. And I'm compelled to remind you, too, that long before most professional editors begin to fret over the wording and structure of individual sentences of a document, they are subjecting the content of that document to a mental grilling designed to produce concrete answers to questions relating to the following four issues:

> ➢ **Comprehensiveness.** Is the content comprehensive enough and reliable enough to meet whatever audience-oriented objective the document is meant to accomplish?
> ➢ **Relevance.** Is the content *relevant* to the document's objective and to the expectations and needs of the intended readers?
> ➢ **Organization.** Has the content been logically organized and sequenced?
> ➢ **Positioning and focus.** Has the content been appropriately positioned, slanted, and shaped?

Analyzing your answers

I wish I could recommend some simple, sure-fire ways to ensure that you come up with accurate answers to these questions, but I can't. For here we have one of the many situations in writing and editing in which there are no shortcuts and no formulas. You simply have to compare, on the one hand, the ideas and information that are *necessary* in light of your objective and your audience to the ideas and information that you've actually communicated. But I urge you to pay particularly close attention to the last of the preceding questions, because it is in this area—how you position and shape the content—that most documents get off the track.

The core issue here is focus—or, as newspaper reporters in 1950s movies might have described it, your "angle." Information, remember, can be shaped in any number of ways, but it is up to you as your own editor to verify that you have shaped the content to the needs and expectations of your readers. If the topic of your document is, say, bicycles, you want to be sure that the focus, slant, and emphasis of the bicycle-related information is keyed to both the editorial mission of the publication (or the department of the publication you're writing for) and the expectations and knowledge level of the audience. Who, ultimately, is going to be reading all this information about bicycles: a man or woman who runs a bicycle store, or an octogenarian who competes in triathlons? Different spokes for different folks.

Let me tell you about a content-related technique that I found exceptionally helpful during that period of my life when I was churning out three or four magazine articles a month (and didn't have the time to come up with horrid puns, like "different spokes for different folks").

I devised a number-based system (one to four), and I used it to rate the relative importance of all the facts, observations, anecdotes, examples, and asides that constituted the content of the article. If a fact, observation, piece of information, or anecdote in a particular passage was crucial, based on what I understood to be the objective of the article and the expectations and needs of my audience, I'd mark a "1" in the margin. If the idea, image, example, or whatever was relevant but not of life-or-death importance, I would rate it as a "2." And so forth.

One reason this procedure was so useful is that it helped me keep in check a tendency I share with many writers, which is to confuse my own stylistic priorities with the content-related priorities of my audience. Coding the content in this way also made things easier for me if the magazine that had assigned the article was tight for space (or so they *claimed*!) and wanted me to do the unthinkable: to cut down on the length of my article. Low-priority content—"4s"— was the first to go, painful though it may have been for me to sacrifice sentences I had worked so hard and lovingly to stitch together.

SETTING LINE-BY-LINE PRIORITIES

Broadly speaking, the purpose of editing is to enhance the *readability* of a document. But readability as a concept is rather like a stew: It isn't any one thing but, rather, a combination of properties. And the most important of those properties (and in their order of importance) are the following: (1) clarity; (2) conciseness; (3) flow; and (4) vividness. These properties are pretty much self-defining, but let me clarify them, anyway.

- ➤ **Clarity** is best measured by how easy it is for readers to grasp the meaning of what you've written—taking into account, of course, that some topics are more complicated than others and that some readers are more literate, more sophisticated, and more familiar with your topic than other readers.
- ➤ **Conciseness** means *economy* of words: getting your message across clearly without burdening your readers with irrelevant information or excess verbiage.
- ➤ **Flow** is a function of how smoothly the writing moves *within* each sentence and from one sentence to the next.

➤ **Vividness** is the capacity of the writing to spark and sustain the interest of your reader—and, if it's part of your objective, to get them excited or emotionally caught up in what you're writing about.

First things first

A quick observation about the properties I've listed above, and the brief description that follows each of them: My intent here is not to set forth The Definitive Theory of How Editing Influences the Readability of a Document. Nor do the categories or their descriptions do justice to the complexity of the properties they embody.

But keeping these four properties of readability in mind as you edit, and, more important, using the sequence I have indicated as a basis of setting priorities, could make you a more *efficient* editor. Instead of prowling through the manuscript in search of "problems" in general, you now have the option of performing your line-by-line editing tasks in precisely targeted stages. You can focus first on how *clearly* the content in a particular passage is being communicated, then on how *concisely* the content is being communicated and, finally (assuming you have the time), on how *smoothly* the writing is moving, or how vividly the ideas and images are being expressed.

True, if you have years of front-line experience under your editing belt, you can usually compress these diverse considerations into a single decision-making process. And even if you follow this sequence, you don't have to be a slave to it. If, while focusing on clarity, you notice a phrase that is clearly redundant, dump it. And regardless of which property (clarity, conciseness, etc.) you're focusing on, if you suddenly come up with a better or livelier way to express an idea, go ahead and make the change.

Bear in mind, though, that given how the human brain likes to operate, we tend to be much more efficient in our cognitive efforts when we can focus on one specific problem at a time, rather than trying to uncover and solve a *range* of problems in one fell swoop. Moreover, as you read through the chapters that lie ahead, you will see that the various tools of editing tend to be keyed to only one of these four properties. Remember, finally, that I'm not asking you to spend *more* time editing your own work than you may now be spending— only to use that time more strategically.

PROOFREADING: EQUAL BUT SEPARATE

There comes a time in the life of every document when somebody (or some software package) has to go through it line by line and word by word to make sure that the document is "clean"— free of misspellings, typos, missing words, and glaring grammar glitches. In most professional situations, this grueling task—usually referred to as "proofreading," but sometimes lumped together with "copyediting"—generally gets handled by someone *other* than the person who wrote or edited the document. And the person to whom this task has been delegated is usually, though not always, endowed with the sweat-nickels-over-the-small stuff temperament you need to be endowed with in order to be a top-gun proofreader.

You may not be blessed with such a temperament, and may not be in a position to delegate this last, but critical, step in the editing process to somebody more temperamentally qualified than you to handle it. This being the case, the following advice might be helpful.

Spell-checkers: trust, but verify

Assuming you use a computer, you would be crazy not to take advantage of whatever spell-checking add-ons might come bundled with your word processing package, albeit with the following caveat: Never put your blind faith in these programs. Software-driven editing devices are terrific at ferreting out misspellings and repeated words, but they are all but useless when it comes to noticing when words have been inadvertently omitted. And none has any way of knowing whether you meant to write *there, their,* or *they're,* or *its,* or *it's.* It's not there [*sic*] job.

Tricks of the trade

A few other practices that might improve your batting average when you proofread:

> ➤ Use a ruler or any opaque object to isolate each line you proofread from the lines that precede or follow.
> ➤ Read the document out of sequence (i.e., start at the end of the document and work your way to the front, paragraph by paragraph).
> ➤ Read the document aloud and do it very, very, very slowly.

Each of these steps in its own way will remind your brain that you're not *reading,* but *proof*reading, which, in turn, may prevent your brain from doing what it sometimes does when you're proofreading, which is to "fill in the blanks" when a word or two is missing from the text.

But probably the best overall advice I can offer on a topic that I am not terribly qualified to offer advice on is this: Treat proofreading as a stage *distinct* from everything else you do as an editor. Set aside enough time (at the very minimum, 60 seconds for each typewritten page), and don't give the process short shrift. Don't shoot yourself in the foot by getting careless at the last moment.

HOW "GOOD" SHOULD IT GET?

It's a given that any document destined to be read by anyone other than you should meet a baseline threshold for clarity and grammatical appropriateness—even if it's a note to your exterminator. But once this threshold has been reached, you need to come to grips with the following question: How "good" does the writing really have to be? At what point, in other words, and after how much time, sweat, nail-biting do you declare your job as editor "finished?"

You shouldn't be in a hurry to answer this question, simply because the question doesn't lend itself to a hurried answer. How well edited a document *needs* to be hinges on several factors, chief among them where it's being published, who's going to be reading it, and how important it is to you personally that the document meet certain standards. An essay on esthetics earmarked for *The American Scholar* is one thing. The minutes of last week's meeting of your local motorcycle club are something else again. Not that your local motorcycle club members are chopped liver. It's simply that you're not going to be drummed out of the club because a some of the sentences in last week's minutes lacked grace and balance—not unless one of the things you do at your motorcycle club meetings is to rhapsodize about the stylistic nuances of James Joyce

Don't get me wrong. I'm not suggesting that you "dumb down" your writing so as not to intimidate readers who are not of your—how shall I put this?—intellectual caliber. And I certainly don't want to rob you of whatever pleasure it may bring you to come up with epiphany-producing analogies or metaphors, and then to express those epiphany-producing analogies or metaphors in beautifully crafted sentences.

So, by all means, set whatever Joycean standards you want to set for yourself when you edit. Just make sure that you stay anchored to Planet Earth, that you strive for these Olympian standards on *your* dime, and that you focus first on the standards that *need* to be met, in light of your audience and your objective.

And one final word of advice: Try to keep your own stylistic idiosyncrasies—your penchant for quirky wording, oddly configured sentences, or n-o-Ve-l w-a-Y-s to format words—from sabotaging your reader's efforts to figure out what in the name of Harley-Davidson you are trying to communicate to them. There may well be an appreciative audience for the individual flourishes that distinguish *your* writing style from other writers; but you are more likely to find such an audience among the people who subscribe to the *New World Quarterly of Really Imaginative Writing from Writers Whose Genius Nobody Really Appreciates* than among the people who normally read what you write. If you can dazzle your readers with your writing style, do it. Just don't blind them in the process.

3

Bone Up on the Fundamentals

When Winston Churchill applied to the English public school Harrow at the age of twelve, he scored so poorly on the Latin and math portions of his entrance examination that he wasn't permitted to take Latin and Greek, but was forced instead to learn the basics of what he sardonically refers to in his autobiography, *My Early Years,* as "that most disregarded thing—how to write mere English." This meant, among other things, that Churchill and his "fellow dunces" were subjected to a daily regimen of sentence-parsing drills during which they used different-colored markers to differentiate the various components of a sentence. It also meant, Churchill tells us, that he eventually got the essential structure of the ordinary English sentence into his "bones." And it ultimately meant that Churchill came to enjoy in his later life what he considered an "immense advantage" over those students at Harrow who had won prizes for their Latin poetry and Greek epigrams, but were eventually forced to "come down again to common English to earn their living or make their way." No surprise, then, to find Churchill advocating in his autobiography that all British schoolboys, regardless of how well they perform on their entrance examinations, should be forced to master the fundamentals of English. "I would let the clever ones learn Latin as an honour and Greek as a treat," he writes. "But the only thing I

21

would whip them for would be not knowing English. I would whip them hard for that."

THE FUNDAMENTALS: A CLOSER LOOK

Is it time to reintroduce corporal punishment (ruler slaps across the knuckles and that sort of thing) for grade-schoolers who can't tell an adjective from an adverb, who habitually dangle participles, and who flagrantly violate the rules of subject-verb agreement?

Probably not. But it is not unreasonable to wonder how much more readable the general level of writing throughout America might be if more of us in *our* early years had gone through the same regimen of sentence-parsing drills that Churchill went through at Harrow. Granted, a "bone-deep" understanding of sentence structure will not itself make you a writer worth reading. But a solid grounding in the basics of sentence structure will surely make you a more knowledgeable—and more confident— editor.

Basic questions

Now for the fundamental question: How deeply embedded in *your* bones do the basics of sentence structure need to be to enable you to operate effectively as your own editor?

I would answer as follows: more deeply embedded, certainly, than it is in non-writers, but not as deeply embedded as it was in Winston Churchill. I see no practical value, for instance, in being able to differentiate—as Churchill could— the various types of clauses (relative, conditional, conjunctive, etc.). But basic sentence literacy obliges you to understand, at the very least, the difference between a phrase and a clause; between a simple sentence, a complex sentence, and a compound sentence; and between a verb and its grammatical cousins—the gerund, infinitive, and participle.

So, here's a down-and-dirty way to get some insight into how much you yourself need to bone up on the fundamentals. I have assembled six questions, each of which touches upon a basic concept of sentence structure, and each of which takes a simple "yes" or "no" answer. If you can answer a resounding "yes" to all the questions, you can relax: You know enough about the basics to recognize and capitalize on the rationale behind the vast majority of the editing decisions you need to make.

If, however, you are baffled by more than one of these questions, there are two ways you can respond. On the one hand, you can keep on reading, and try to get a sense of these concepts on the fly (and I've done my best not to get too technical in the chapters that follow). On the other hand, you might want to think about getting hold of a grammar primer, the idea being to acquaint (or reacquaint) yourself with the basic concepts of sentence structure.

No wincing, please. Grim though the prospect of revisiting the fundamentals of sentence structure may seem, it shouldn't take you very long—a few hours at most—to get your arms around the basic concepts. We are not dealing here, remember, with quantum physics. And whatever time you invest in this process will deepen your understanding of editing, and will more than pay for itself in the long run.

Pencils ready? Here goes:

> ➤ Can you look at a fairly complex sentence and identify its primary parts—*subject, verb,* and *complement?*
>
> ➤ Do you know the difference between a *phrase* and a *clause,* and what impact this difference has on how much emphasis is accorded to the information or image that is conveyed in one or the other?
>
> ➤ Do you know the difference between a *dependent clause* (also known as *subordinate clause)* and an *independent clause?*
>
> ➤ Do you know the dif ference between a *simple sentence,* a *complex sentence,* and a *compound sentence?* (Hint: It has

23

nothing do with how "simple" or "complex" the idea is.) And can you explain why you might choose to use one instead of the other?

➤ Do you know the difference between essential elements in a sentence (also known as *restrictive* elements) and nonessential elements, and why this difference matters so much in punctuation and the choice between *that* or *which*?

➤ Do you understand the difference between a verbal and a true verb—and why that difference can affect how smoothly a sentence flows and how logically an introductory phrase relates to the main thought of the sentence?

The envelope, please

Here's a crash course in the concepts mentioned in the preceding questions:

Subject, verb, complement. The *subject* is a word or group of words that represents the specific person, place, thing, or idea a sentence or a clause is talking about. The *verb* is the word that (1) expresses the action the subject is taking; or (2) joins with another word to describe the subject's state of being. The *complement* is the word or group of words usually needed to complete the thought partially formed by the subject and its verb.

Significance. In a typical English sentence, the subject *precedes* the verb, and the complement *follows* the verb. You can—and should—vary this structure from time to time; but however you vary it, the subject, verb, and complement should always be the building blocks of your sentences, and should also be prominent enough so that your readers can easily identify each component. The reason? Until they can figure out which words in any sentence are filling these critical roles, your readers have no way of distilling any meaning from the sentence. More on this point in Chapter 9.

Phrases versus clauses. A *phrase* is simply a group of related words that operate more or less as a unit. A *clause* is a group of words that contain at least one subject-verb tandem.

Significance. Knowing the difference between phrases and clauses helps you control the shading of your sentences—that is, how much emphasis is accorded to each of the ideas and images you've expressed in a sentence. Everything else equal, ideas expressed in clauses carry more weight than ideas expressed in phrases (Chapter 13).

Independent clauses and subordinate clauses. An *independent clause* can stand alone as a completed thought. A *dependent* or *subordinate clause* needs to be linked with an independent clause to complete the thought.

Significance. If an idea and image is of primary importance to the message you want to get across, your impulse should be to express it in an independent clause, as opposed to a dependent clause or a phrase. And whenever you come across a complex sentence (see next item), you want to be sure that the idea expressed in the dependent clause is indeed subordinate to the idea expressed in the independent clause.

Categorizing sentences. Sentences can be classified in one of three ways, based on their grammatical DNA. A *simple sentence* consists of only one subject-verb tandem, never mind how long the sentence is, or how much information it conveys. A *complex sentence* is any sentence with two or more clauses, one of which is dependent. (Here, again, it isn't its length or the complexity of its subject matter that determines whether a sentence is "complex"—it's the number and nature of the clauses.) A *compound sentence* consists of two independent clauses that are usually linked by a conjunction, such as *and, but,* or *because.*

Significance. The *kinds* of sentences you use throughout a document invariably affect the pace and the flow of the writing.

Skilled writers are comfortable with all three sentence types, but tend to rely primarily on simple sentences.

Essential and nonessential clauses and phrases. Clauses and phrases are "essential" (the technical term is "restrictive") when removing them from the sentence will either obscure or distort the meaning of the content. A clause or phrase is "nonessential" when, after having removed it from the sentence, the main idea is still intact and logical.

Significance. The difference between essential and nonessential sentence elements is the core issue in two common editing decisions: (1) whether you set the element apart from the rest of the sentence with commas (essential clause or phrase: no; nonessential clause or phrase: yes); (2) whether you use *which* or *that* (general rule: *that* for essential clauses and phrases; *which* for nonessential).

Verbs and verbals. Verbals are grammatical forms (*gerunds, infinitives,* and *participles*) that are built around verbs but operate as modifiers, which means that they don't have a subject. The key reason it helps to know what verbals are and how they differ from true verbs is to avoid "dangling" modifiers (Chapter 8). But this knowledge will also help you make better use of the writing and editing technique known as parallel structure (Chapter 17).

4

Make Sure the Words Say What You Want Them to Mean

When my grandson Jeremy was three and we took him out to eat, he always asked for "yayas." "Yayas"—he p r onounced it "yahyahs"—was Jeremy-talk for french-fried potatoes. But other than the fact that "Yayas" is part of the title of a Rolling Stones song, I have no idea why he chose such an un-french-fried-potato-like sounding word to express his favorite food.

Then again, it didn't matter—certainly not to Jeremy. *He* always had a clear idea of what he wanted to eat when he asked for "yayas." And because he was invariably surrounded by people who granted him unlimited linguistic license, he always got what he asked for. The only thing I had to be careful about was that I didn't slip into Jeremy-talk when I placed the order. If I were a harried counter person at a McDonald's or Burger King, and someone taller than a counter stool requested "yayas," my impulse would be to dial 911.

THE "YAYA" EFFECT IN WRITING

Nearly all of us, to varying degrees, do in our writing what my grandson used to do when he hankered for french fries. Simply put, we don't pay sufficient attention to how precisely we choose our words. We assume that as long as the words we've chosen to express our ideas give our readers a ballpark approximation of the idea we're trying to get across, our readers will be smart enough—and hungry enough for the idea— to puzzle out for themselves what we're trying to tell them.

This can be a risky assumption, to say the least. Consider what happened several years ago when a hotel manager in Mexico, seeking to reassure his guests that the hotel's water supply was safe to drink, wrote the following message on a sign that he posted in the hotel restaurant: "The water here is safe to drink. It has been personally passed by the manager."

Or consider a sentence I came across many years ago in a student essay written by a young woman whose house had become infested with ants. In her efforts to solve the problem, the woman had gone on a spraying binge, concentrating in particular on the tiny cracks in the woodwork where the ants were streaming in from the outside. But here is how she described those efforts: "I've done everything in my power to get rid of the ants. I've even sprayed them in their private places."

WHY WORDS CAN'T BE TRUSTED

Their unintended comic effects apart, the preceding examples of mixed signals in communication drive home a basic but insufficiently appreciated truth not only about writing but also about communication in general. They remind us that words have no intrinsic meaning; they're simply symbols, a form of code. As such, words serve no productive function until somebody (a listener or a reader) decodes them into the thoughts or images that were the wellsprings of those words in the first place.

More to the point, these examples and dozens of others I could cite, remind us that English is a minefield of ambiguity, and that it is booby-trapped throughout with words and phrases whose meanings can be inferred in myriad ways, depending on context and the audience's frame of reference. These examples underscore, finally, how easy it is to create confusion in the minds of your readers when you don't pay enough attention to word choice during writing, and when you don't bail yourself out during editing.

I can think of no challenge more fundamental to editing your own work than the challenge implicit in the observation I've just made: verifying that the words you've chosen as the "code" for your ideas can be successfully "decoded" by your readers. And given the fact that you already know, having chosen the words yourself, what ideas or images the words are *meant* to convey, I can think of no challenge in self-editing more difficult to meet.

There is, however, at least one strategy I can suggest that, at the very least, will heighten your sensitivity to "yayas" in your own writing. And that is to be especially alert to the Big Enchilada of "yayas," and the number one source of imprecision in writing. It is a syndrome that Donald Hall refers to in *Writing Well* as "lazy abstractions."

LAZY ABSTRACTIONS DEFINED

A "lazy abstraction," as Hall defines the term, is a word or phrase that sort of, kind of expresses the idea or image you want to get across, but is neither concrete enough nor precise enough to create a specific picture of that idea or image where it matters the most: in your reader's mind. Your readers can sometimes figure out for themselves what idea or image a lazy abstraction is meant to get across, but their ability to do so depends on their frame of reference and, more important, on how hard your readers are willing to work. Lazy readers and lazy abstractions are a lethal combination.

"Private places"—the example I used earlier—is a classic example of a lazy abstraction. In the mind's eye of the writer, "private places" were those cracks in the woodwork that the ants in her house were using as their private entrances. But even in the context of pest control, "private places" doesn't *say* "cracks in the woodwork that ants use as their private entrances." "Private places" can mean any number of things, some of them a good deal racier than the writer had in mind.

Which is the basic problem of lazy abstractions. Lacking specificity, they do not *control* the association that readers draw from them. Here's an innocent example:

> In light of **personnel fluctuations** over the past several months, the company has had to reevaluate its training procedures.

Okay, you sort of, kind of get what the writer is trying to say here. The company's work force has obviously been in flux in recent months—veteran employees leaving, new people coming aboard. But that's not what "personnel fluctuations" *says*. Personnel do not "fluctuate." Temperatures and interest rates fluctuate. What the writer *ought* to have written here is something more akin to the following:

> In light of ~~personnel fluctuations~~ the **unusually high rate of employee turnover** in recent months, the company has had to reevaluate its training procedures.

Granted, my edited version is slightly longer than the original. But what's the point of brevity if the reader doesn't know what you're talking about? What matters most in reading is not the number of *words* the reader has to process, but how long it takes to *process* those words.

Here's yet another example of this syndrome—this one not quite so innocent since it comes from a widely read business journal.

Make way for the new way of business: Information technologies are going to make emotions a regular feature of business.

As it happens, I once met with the man who wrote this sentence, and so I was able get firsthand clarification on what he was driving at when he wrote that information technologies are going to make "emotions a regular feature of business." His point (and he shared it with me with obvious impatience, as though *any* moron would know what he meant) was this: that the rapidly expanding multi-media capabilities of desktop computers will enable businesses in the future to incorporate dramatic sound effects and striking visual images in their presentations and, by doing so, will be able to generate more emotional impact. Silly me for asking.

LAZY ABSTRACTIONS: A CASE STUDY

One of the most striking (and instructive) examples I've ever seen of what can happen when a paragraph is infested with lazy abstractions comes from a student essay I first came across nearly twenty years ago. The writer, a man in his early thirties, had a promising idea for this essay: He wanted to convince his readers that it is far more interesting to go food shopping in the small, privately owned grocery stores typically found in ethnic neighborhoods than it is to shop in the typical suburban supermarket—and mainly because of the *aromatic* dimension of the experience. Consider, though, how he chose to put this idea into words:

> The art of smelling is rapidly declining due to the advent of cellophane products, but smelling is still to be found in precincts where grocery stores maintain their ethnic aromas.

This sentence talks about a lot of things: "smelling," "cellophane products," "grocery stores," and "ethnicity." The key question, though, is this: What, in fact, are the words throughout this sentence really *saying*? What ideas and images, in other words, do they produce in your mind as you read them?

Let's start with the first clause:

The art of smelling is rapidly declining

What does the phrase "art of smelling" mean? And once you've come up with an answer, here's another question: what is it about this "art" that is "declining"?

Neither question lends itself to smack-you-in-the-forehead answer. "Smelling," strictly speaking, means one of two things: (1) to detect an odor, as in, "I can smell the toast burning," or (2) to emit an odor, as in, "Does my breath smell funny?"

Okay, when you're talking about people who create perfume scents, smelling might be classified as an "art." Most folks, though, associate "art" with pursuits like cooking, sculpting, flower arranging, karate, or tuba playing, and smelling doesn't make the cut. Smelling doesn't have its own muse, or its own tax-exempt foundation. And because there is no way of knowing for certain what the writer meant by the "art" of smelling, we have no way of knowing what he meant when he told us this "art" is on the decline.

Look now at the next phrase:

due to the advent of cellophane products

The writer probably meant to write *"cellophaned* products," and no doubt had in mind fruits, meats, and vegetables wrapped in cellophane. Either way, though, the phrase is too vague. How could we possibly know what image he had in mind: cellophaned-wrapped mangos, or cellophaned-wrapped flashlight batteries?

Let's go on:

but smelling is still to be found in precincts where
grocery stores maintain their ethnic aromas.

I don't know about you, but the image that came to *my* mind
the first time I read "smelling is still to be found" is that of a pack of
supermarket shoppers sniffing their way through the aisles like those
German shepherds they deploy at airports to sniff out contraband
drugs—probably not the image the reader had in mind.

"Ethnic aromas?"

Is the writer suggesting that if you were to walk into a room
with your eyes closed but your nostrils clear, you would be able to
tell, simply by inhaling, whether the room was filled with Italians
or Greeks or Germans? I hope not.

If you think I'm being picky, you're right. But I am not unbiased
in these matters. I happen to believe, simply, that if you expect
someone to read something you've written, it's your responsibility—
nay, your sacred mission!—to choose words that accurately convey
what you're trying to say. It's okay to fall back on lazy abstractions
as interim coding devices when you're first getting your thoughts
down on paper. But by the time a document is ready to be *edited*, all
such imprecision should have been cleared up. The sentence we've
been picking on fails to meet the fundamental standard of effective
writing: It doesn't *say* what it's supposed to *mean*.

Editing your way out of imprecision

Had this particular writer been more sensitive to the needs of
his readers, and therefore less prone to lazy abstractions, he might
have written this paragraph in the following way:

> Now that supermarkets have begun to package
> nearly all their meats, produce, and baked goods
> in cellophane, it is becoming harder than ever to

take advantage of your sense of smell when you go food shopping. But you can still enjoy the aromatic aspect of food shopping when you patronize the small grocery stores in ethnic neighborhoods.

To be sure, it has taken more than simple line-editing to produce this revision. The original sentence, in fact, has been rewritten. So be it. The only way to deal with lazy abstractions when you edit is to replace them with words or phrases that spell out what you are trying to say. And whether you want to describe that move as an "edit" or a "rewrite," it doesn't matter. Somebody has to do it; and, as your own editor, that somebody is you.

LAZY ABSTRACTIONS, PROFESSIONAL STYLE

Lazy abstractions are not the sole province of student writers. A case in point is the following example, which I plucked recently from an architectural magazine. The ostensible purpose of the paragraph was to point out that artists, on the whole, do not concern themselves with the long-term physical durability of their works. Here's how the sentence appeared in print:

Most artists have little consideration for the longevity of their works, whose deterioration depends on the materials used, the conditions they are subjected to, and occasionally, the tampering that they endure.

As we saw in the "ethnic aromas" paragraph, the words used to express the ideas in this sentence are far too vague. Here's another look at the paragraph, but this time with the lazy abstractions set apart in bold face, and ambiguity discussed in the right-hand column.

Most artists **have little consideration** for the **longevity of their works,**	"Have little consideration" could mean one of two things: (1) are inconsiderate of; or (2) don't give much thought to.
whose **deterioration depends on the materials being** used	"Deterioration" doesn't *depend* on anything: it's *produced* or *caused* by something.
...the **conditions they are subjected** to	What "conditions"? Environmental, temperature, economic, etc.
...and the **tampering** they endure.	What sort of "tampering"? Who is doing it? Is it intentional or inadvertent, malicious or well-intentioned?

Had this paragraph been written or edited more carefully, the vaguely worded phrases that appear in boldface in the left-handed column might have been replaced with the more precisely chosen words in the right-hand column.

...have **little consideration for** the **longevity of their works, whose deterioration depends on the materials being** used	pay little attention to whether the materials they use in their works will withstand.

...the **conditions they are sub-jected** to	the environmental conditions (temperature, heat, humidity, etc.) that works of art are often exposed to.
...and the **tampering** they endure.	the damaging things that people—innocently or otherwise— will sometimes do to to a work of art.

These replacements having been made, the paragraph might well have read as follows:

> Most artists ~~have little consideration for the longevity of their works, whose deterioration depends on the materials being used, the conditions they are subjected to~~ **pay little attention to whether the materials they use in their works will withstand the environmental conditions (temperature, heat, humidity, etc.) that works of art are often exposed to.** ~~and the tampering that they endure.~~ **And most artists rarely stop to think about all the damaging things that people— innocently or otherwise—will sometimes do to a work of art.**

Once again the edited version is lengthier than the original, but we can always trim it—now that we've taken care of the most important priority: clarity.

SUMMING UP

Choosing words that communicate—with precision!— what you want those words to *mean* requires no special talent or skill. But it does require discipline, motivation, and a strong sense of obligation to your readers.

To find out if you rely too much on lazy abstractions when you write, here's a suggestion: Get hold of a document you've written recently—perhaps an article that you haven't been able to get published—and go through the text line by line, stopping after each sentence to ask yourself the following question: "Do the words in this sentence explicitly express the idea or image I want to convey?"

Don't answer the question too quickly. Put yourself in the shoes of somebody who knows next to nothing about the subject you're talking about, and ask yourself whether the words you've chosen will re-create in that person's mind the specific idea or image you want to get across.

Better still, find somebody who doesn't know beans about the subjects you write about and doesn't worship the ground you walk on. Ask that person to read a random group of sentences (don't worry if the sentences are out of context: that's the whole point of the exercise) and to tell you in his or her own words what idea or image comes to *their* mind in each of sentences you've asked them to read. What you're looking for is a perfect match. If you don't get a perfect match, don't blame the reader. Blame yourself for being too abstract—and too lazy.

5

"Umbrella-ize" the Ideas in Your Paragraphs

E diting with an eye toward clarity would be a piece of cake if you could go about your business the same way you tidy up your house or apartment. You could walk into each individual sentence (so to speak), straighten out whatever mess you found, and then move on to the next sentence. You would never have to look back, or ahead. And you could take comfort in the knowledge that as long as everything was shipshape in the sentences you've just cleaned up, the document as a whole would eventually take care of itself.

So much for wishful thinking. The fact is, editing for clarity *isn't* like tidying up your house or apartment, the chief reason being that the individual sentences in a typical document do not operate in a vacuum. Yes, each sentence you edit needs to pull its own weight: links in a chain, and all that. But how clearly you communicate the information you want to get across in your documents is determined only marginally by how clearly the information is expressed in individual sentences. The litmus test is what happens when readers do what readers are programmed to do, which is to try to distill meaning from the collective content of individual sentences.

THE TWO FACES OF CLARITY

To give you a better sense of the distinction I am drawing here between clarity as it relates to individual sentences, and clarity as it relates to ideas coming together to form coherent thoughts, I invite you to read the following paragraph. It comes from a memo written by a computer specialist, and I should warn you up front: The paragraph could be hazardous to your reading health.

> At the request of Phil Jennings, of Human Resources, a program relating to the Technical Talent Survey was recently written on the system specifying one or more technical talents. The file used as input has all the information about the Technical Talent Survey, which was sent to employees concerning their talents, education, and career goals. All people do not express similar talents in the same way. The original program had an inflexible search feature. To use the new program, you can type in from one to fifteen letters for each talent.

I often use this paragraph in my writing seminars. I have the class members read it to themselves, and once they've read it, I ask them to write out a sentence that summarizes what they think the paragraph is "about." I then record the class responses on a flip chart.

You can probably guess what happens. The statements on the list that eventually fills the flip chart all allude in one way or another to "talent survey," but they invariably reflect a hodgepodge of interpretations. What the exercise clearly demonstrates is that a paragraph can be filled with individual sentences that make perfectly good sense on their own, but fail, as a group, to communicate a coherent idea—or, as I choose to call it, an umbrella thought.

Time now to shift gears. In merciful contrast to the paragraph you've just read, the paragraph that follows is an excellent—if exaggerated—example of a paragraph in which clarity works on both a sentence-by-sentence level *and* a paragraph level. The paragraph comes from a book entitled *The Haphazard Gourmet,* by the late journalist, Richard Gehman.

> The fact is, I make good gravy. I never miss. I am the Uncontested Gravy Champion of the United States, Europe, Asia, Australia and—I think—Africa. I have never been to Africa, except to Egypt, which doesn't count, but I am almost dead certain that nobody there could possibly make gravy as well as I do. As soon as we get to the moon, I will be Moon Gravy Champion, too. Cookbooks are going to leave their gravy sections blank simply because their writers will know how useless it would be to attempt to describe any gravy but mine.

You may not appreciate Richard Gehman's sense of humor; and you may question whether he needed to remind us as often—and in as many ways—of his gravy-making studmanship.

But the one thing you *can't* say about this paragraph is that it fails to communicate a clear, coherent umbrella thought. Information abounds in this paragraph, but it all relates to one thought—the fact that, as he sees it, Richard Gehman is *the* man when it comes to making gravy.

UMBRELLA-IZING AS AN EDITING STRATEGY

If you want the umbrella thought concept to work for you as an editing tool, you need to be able to do something that is by no means easy to do, which is to anticipate what is going on in your readers' minds as they move from one sentence to the next in your paragraphs. And you need to remember at the same time, that although *you* may be aware of what umbrella thought a paragraph was meant to get across, your readers have nothing to go on but the words they encounter in each sentence.

One reliable—though admittedly cumbersome—way to gain some insight into whether your writing has the coherency that umbrella-izing your ideas can bring to it is to go through a procedure that actually "tracks" the thought pattern likely to materialize in the minds of your readers as they move from sentence to sentence.

Here's how the procedure works: You take a paragraph you have written that consists of at least four or five sentences. You then read each sentence one by one, and you jot down in the margin—and in the broadest of terms—what general thought that particular piece of information is communicating.

You need to take your time when you do this, and you need to discipline yourself to record in the margin not what the sentence *ought* to be saying but what the words in the sentence are *actually* saying. You also want to pay particularly close attention to any abrupt shifts in *mode*—whether, for example, the writing shifts without warning from a *description* of something to a *command* or *suggestion*.

If you were to perform this exercise with the "technical talent survey" paragraph, the first three or four notes might look like the list that follows, and you would recognize right away that the ideas are not "tracking."

➢ Request for a program relating to Technical talent survey
➢ File sent to employees
➢ How people express talents
➢ Original program inflexible

The pattern of margin notes would be noticeably different, though, if you were to perform the same exercise on the Gehman paragraph. Each note would echo the same idea— that Gehman makes great gravy.

Let us look at how this exercise might work with a paragraph from a student paper:

> Speaker credibility has been discussed and investigated for 2500 years. We have all experienced speaking and listening to other people and as a result we have believed or disbelieved what was said. What is it that makes us believe or disbelieve a person? Aristotle, 2300 years ago, cited three qualities: good sense, good moral character, and good will.

Here, as in the earlier paragraph, we're confronted with a "tracking" problem. The paragraph is obviously about "credibility" but the focus jumps around from sentence to sentence. It starts with a fact, and then jumps abruptly to an observation, followed by a question and its answer. The result: there is no umbrella thought. If you were a professional editor and you came across this paragraph, or the "talent survey" example that preceded it, you would probably bump it back to the writer. If you had written either of these paragraphs yourself, you would have no choice: you would have to bump it back to yourself.

Solving the problem

So the question now becomes, what do you do when you come across a paragraph in which the information doesn't coalesce into an umbrella thought? The answer is not as mysterious as you may think. You need to determine *what* thought you want the paragraph to convey, and you need to make subsequent editing decisions accordingly.

This answer may seem too simplistic to be practical. But let us assume that the writer of the technical talent survey paragraph and the writer of the "credibility" paragraph had each taken the "umbrella thought" approach I am advocating here. This means that they would have taken a moment or so *before* they wrote or edited the paragraph to determine what umbrella thought they wanted the paragraph to convey.

In the "talent survey" example, the writer would have probably determined that what he was really talking about in this paragraph was not simply a new software program that had been written. It was really about a *problem* that he had been called upon to solve. With this umbrella thought etched in his mind, he would have probably recognized the need to *identify* the problem, and then to describe the steps taken to *correct* it. And given this mental framework (a problem and a solution) the paragraph he eventually wrote might have looked—fingers crossed!—like this:

> One of the things we were asked to do this month was to help Phil Jennings of Human Resources solve a tracking problem that has arisen in connection with the program we developed for the new Technical Talent Survey.
>
> The problem we were asked to solve relates to the inability of the individual records in Technical Talent Survey program to provide enough data to make the program efficient to use. Each record lists the talent, education, and career goals of each employee. But what we did not take into account when we wrote this program was the fact that not all people use the same wording to express the same talent. And the search capabilities we developed for the system were not flexible enough to account for these differences.
>
> We have tried to solve this problem by increasing the capabilities of the search utilities. Users will now be able to search talents on the basis of up to fifteen characters.

It's not by accident that this edited version reads far more clearly and coherently than the jumble of ideas that I threw at you in the original version. We're told in the first sentence what thought the reader wants to get across—that a program has been created to solve a problem; and each of the next two paragraphs has its own umbrella thought. The umbrella thought in the second paragraph is the "problem." In the third paragraph, it's the "solution."

Let's look now at how this same principle might apply to the "credibility" paragraph. As I see it, the writer needs to do just two things in this paragraph: pose a rhetorical question about credibility and then answer it with an observation by Aristotle. Look now at how much more cohesively the paragraph reads when this pattern becomes the umbrella thought.

> Speaker credibility has been discussed and investigated for 2500 years, **but why is it, exactly, that we believe what some people tell us and disbelieve what others tell us?** ~~We have all experienced speaking and listening to other people and as a result we have believed or disbelieved what was said. What is it that makes us believe or disbelieve a person?~~ Aristotle, 2300 years ago, **answered this question in terms of** ~~cited~~ three qualities: good sense, good moral character, and good will.

Is this brilliant writing? Hardly. But the paragraph, unlike the original, makes sense. Later in the book, we will be looking at some other tools that, in concert with umbrella-izing, can go a long way to unify the information in paragraphs that lack cohesion. For now, though, keep in mind the basic principle. Before you start to worry about how clearly information is being communicated on a sentence-by-sentence basis, ask yourself what umbrella thought the information in each sentence tying into. If the answer isn't apparent to *you*, you can be certain that your readers won't be able to figure it out, either.

6

Let Your Readers Know What's Coming

One of the simplest ways to reinforce the "umbrella-izing" effect I brought to your attention in the preceding chapter also happens to be one of the most obvious. Maybe too obvious. You simply begin the paragraph with a sentence that comes right out and *announces* the umbrella thought. Here are two paragraphs—the first from David McCullough's biography of Harry Truman, and the second from an essay by P. J. O'Rourke—that illustrate the kind of announcement I'm talking about:

> DAVID MCCULLOUGH
> For Democrats everywhere it was a dismal time. At the national convention in New York's Madison Square Garden the delegates took a record 103 ballots to pick an unknown, unlikely Wall Street lawyer as their candidate for President, John W. Davis, who seemed destined to lose. A drive to nominate the colorful Catholic governor of New York, Al Smith, had failed along with a resolution to denounce the Ku Klux Klan. And when William Jennings Bryan

tried to speak, he was rudely shouted down. To the Jackson County delegation, it was a pathetic show.

P. J. O'ROURKE

Moscow has changed. I was here in 1982, during the Brezhnev twilight, and things are better now. For instance, they've got litter. In 1982, there was nothing to litter with. People in the street don't dress like the cast in an amateur production of Guys and Dolls any more, and they've quit cutting their hair with tin snips. Only the little kids stare at foreigners. There are more cars. Rush hour in Moscow is almost like 9:00 A.M. on a Sunday morning in Manhattan. The food is hugely improved. True, there was something called "jullienne of meat" on my hotel dinner menu, but I'm pretty sure it was meat from a recognized domestic animal killed during recent history—and it was edible.

The technical term for a sentence that comes at the beginning of a paragraph and tells the reader what the paragraph is going to be about is "topic sentence." I prefer the term "umbrella sentence." "Umbrella" is more—well, visual. It does a better job of conveying what such a sentence is meant to do—to "umbrella-ize" the information that follows.

Whatever you choose to call such sentences, though, the concept hardly exemplifies out-of-the-box thinking. You were probably introduced to this writing tool, in fact, when you were in the fifth grade, which might explain why you go out of your way *not* to begin your paragraphs with this type of sentence. You view this device as being too "remedial"—the writing equivalent of training wheels. You worry that if you begin a paragraph with a sentence that actually *tells* your readers what idea you want to get across, your readers will feel as though you are patronizing them and will take offense.

Fear not. Far from feeling patronized or insulted when they come across an opening sentence that spells out the overall thought of the paragraph, most readers—especially those who have gone through speed-reading courses—will be grateful, and why not? Once readers know what overall thought the paragraph is supposed to convey, they don't have to work as hard to process and distill meaning from the information that follows.

Not that there aren't one or two strings attached to this otherwise straightforward principle. For one thing, you need to be able to recognize when a paragraph could actually *benefit* from an umbrella sentence. And you have to remember, too, that an umbrella sentence is not a magic wand: Sticking an umbrella sentence at the beginning of a paragraph whose content is a disjointed mess is about as intelligent a move as covering a gaping hole in your roof with the front page of the morning paper.

PUTTING UMBRELLA SENTENCES TO WORK

Let's start with when you *don't* usually need an umbrella sentence. You don't normally need an umbrella sentence in paragraphs whose information extends a thought that has been spelled out in the preceding paragraph. Nor do you necessarily need—or want!—an umbrella sentence in a paragraph whose function is simply to narrate a sequence of chronological activities that all relate to the same event, such as what you did on your summer vacation or what you ate and drank last night for dinner.

Sometimes, too—for purposes of humor or suspense—you may want the umbrella thought to gradually unfold in the writer's mind. (This approach to structuring a paragraph is generally known as inductive reasoning, and tends to work better in presentations that it does on the written page.)

When, then, should you be looking to put this technique to work? Primarily in expository writing—and, in particular, in paragraphs in which individual sentences all relate to the same general thought but do not relate very well to each other.

What follows is a classic example of the kind of paragraph that could clearly benefit from an umbrella sentence. It is a slightly doctored version of a course description that appeared in an adult education newsletter. Its purpose was to describe a video production workshop conducted by a woman whom I'll call Mariel Shaw.

> Mariel Shaw's video workshop is run in four intensely paced, all-day sessions. The workshop gives participants hands-on experience with state-of-the-art video equipment. Enrollment is limited to five students. The workshop simulates the pressures and interactions that video production specialists have to deal with in the real world. Ms. Shaw encourages her students to be honest when evaluating their own work and the work of others.

There's nothing egregiously *wrong* with this paragraph. The individual pieces of information about the workshop are easy to understand, and the sentences are reasonably well constructed. Even so, the paragraph seems disjointed and lifeless. Worse, the course sounds as boring as a trip to your local motor vehicle bureau.

The key to bringing more cohesion and more life to this paragraph is not to burrow through your thesaurus in search of livelier *words*. The key is to find a more interesting—and workable—*umbrella thought* for the information. As it happens, there *is* such a thought in this paragraph, and it gets communicated in the fourth sentence. It's the fact that Mariel Shaw's workshops have been expressly designed to mirror the pressure of real-world video production work.

Look at what happens to the readability of this paragraph when that idea becomes the paragraph's umbrella thought— and the basis of an umbrella sentence:

Mariel Shaw's video workshop is ~~run in~~ **designed to simulate the pressures and interactions that video production specialists have to deal with in the real world.** **Each workshop consists of** four intensely paced, all-day sessions. **And to make sure that** ~~The workshops give~~ participants **get** hands-on experience with state-of-the-art video ~~equipment.~~ ~~Enrollment~~ **equipment, enrollment** is limited to five students. ~~The workshop simulates the pressures and interactions that video production specialists have to deal with in the real world.~~ Ms. Shaw also encourages her students to be honest when evaluating their own work and the work of others.

Two points are worth emphasizing about the edits that have produced this paragraph.

Point number one is that the idea expressed in this umbrella sentence is not only broad enough to encompass the information that follows, it is also narrow enough to give that information within a paragraph a point of view. This paragraph is no longer simply *about* the workshop. It's about the *uniqueness* of the workshop—that fact that it simulates the real-world pressures of the video production business.

Point number two is that the umbrella sentence itself is all encompassing: All the information conveyed in each of the sentences falls within the umbr ella of the main thought—the notion of simulating the real-world pressures of video production. That the course runs for four days and is limited to only five students are no longer disembodied bits of information. Feeding as they do into an umbrella thought, these two pieces of information now have a meatier, more meaningful context. True, the paragraph has required some additional tinkering, but fine-tuning of this sort is fairly easy once you've settled upon an umbrella thought.

Let us look now at one last example of how a strong umbrella sentence can imbue a wishy-washy paragraph about a routine subject with more coherency and zip. The original version of the two paragraphs that follow should remind you of the Mariel Shaw paragraph: several pieces of related information that do not hang together very well.

> Real estate appraisers conduct a personal inspection of your home, during which they look at both its interior and exterior condition. Appraisers also take note of the floor plan, and because they are especially interested in the market value of your home, they take into account the "curb appeal" of your property—how impressed potential buyers are likely to be when they drive up and get their first look at the house.

As in the Mariel Shaw paragraph, there's an umbrella thought buried here in the middle of the paragraph. It's the fact that real estate appraisers help home owners determine the market value of their home. Look what happens to the cohesiveness of this paragraph when you use this idea as the basis of an umbrella sentence. Notice, too, as you read through this paragraph, that every sentence in the paragraph ties into the same umbrella idea—*market value*.

> **The main job of real estate appraisers is to help you determine the market value of your home.** ~~Appraisers~~ **They** conduct a personal inspection of your home, and take note of both its interior and exterior condition. ~~Appraisers~~ **They** also take note of the floor plan, ~~because they are especially interested in the market value of your home,~~ and they ~~take into account~~ **are particularly interested in the** "curb appeal" of your property—how impressed potential buyers are likely to be when they drive up to your house.

7

Be Paranoid About Pronouns

P ronouns are those short, ubiquitous words (*he, she, it, they, this*, etc.) whose main job in language is to substitute for words or phrases you would otherwise have to repeat. And given how often we use pronouns, I can't imagine how we could get along without them. If it weren't for pronouns, for example, the previous sentence would have read as follows:

> And given how often every person reading this book uses pronouns, Barry Tarshis can't imagine how every person reading this book could get along without pronouns.

But indispensable though they are, pronouns can be a pesky and frequent source of ambiguity. Because most pronouns have no inherent identity of their own, the mention or sight of them obliges a listener or a reader to link them (the pronouns) with the words or phrases for which they are pinch-hitting. The word, image, or idea the pronoun is standing in for is known as the *antecedent* or *referent*; and in careful writing, the connection between a pronoun and its antecedent is so obvious that readers don't have to think about it. When you came across the phrase "its antecedent" in the previous sentence, for example, you didn't have to put down the book and think to yourself, "Hmm. I wonder what word 'its' is referring to. Oh, I see: the *pronoun's* antecedent. Yes!" The connection took hold instantaneously.

Instant connections are what *should* happen when readers come across a pronoun. But things don't always go according to script. Consider the following sentences:

> The new storage units have become a problem for the managers. They simply do not like the fact that they are being used as trash receptacles.

> The lab workers store the chemicals in a freezer where the temperatures are 30 degrees below zero. They remain there for six months.

> I asked the doctor to examine the bump on my head. When he looked at my head, he said, "It has to come off."

The problem in each of these examples—and the reason we chuckle at them—is that the structure and wording of the sentences induce us to connect the pronouns to words that are not the true referents.

Hence, we're presented with an image of disgruntled managers being heaped with trash, traumatized lab workers being locked up in a freezing warehouse for a year, and a head, rather than a bump, being lopped off as a routine medical procedure.

PRONOUNS AND THE BRAIN

Why the brain, brainy as it is, can't prevent these oddball tandems from forming is anybody's guess. I have a theory, though, and it goes like this:

When readers come face-to-face with a pronoun, two things happen more or less simultaneously inside the reader's brain. One part of the brain keeps moving ahead, gathering in and processing new words. Meanwhile, a different part of the brain goes fishing in short-term memory for the referent. The "continue to read on" component of this split task gets handled by the smarter part of your brain—the part that's calling the shots when you are inventing a new computer code, programming your VCR, or watching *Jeopardy.* The "search for the referent" mission gets handled by the slower part of the brain—that part that's in command when you are boiling water, brushing your teeth, or watching *Wheel of Fortune.*

You will probably never read about this theory in a neuroscience journal—not unless I devote the rest of my life to proving it (the "theory," not the "life"). But unproven though it may be, the theory explains why pronoun/referent connections need to be idiot-proof. For if the referent hasn't been solidly planted in the reader's mind, or if other words in the vicinity might conceivably fool Mother Brain, the usual result is ambiguity, as in this slightly doctored version of a paragraph from a small-town newspaper in Pennsylvania.

> CBS, which lost professional football rights to the Fox network, is expected to program a number of figure-skating competitions against the NFL TV games next fall. It is already making preparations for them. This would be natural since it is showing the Winter Olympic games beginning Feb. 12. It has also secured the rights for them in 1998.

The writer here gives us a vague idea of what CBS is up to, but he doesn't make it easy for us to connect the pronouns to their proper referents. Here's a glimpse of what the "search-for-the-referent" part of the typical reader's brain might be asking itself.

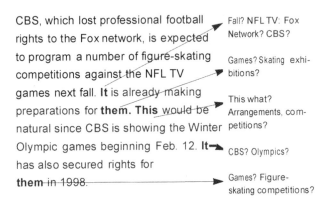

CBS, which lost professional football rights to the Fox network, is expected to program a number of figure-skating competitions against the NFL TV games next fall. **It** is already making preparations for **them**. **This** would be natural since CBS is showing the Winter Olympic games beginning Feb. 12. **It** has also secured rights for **them** in 1998.

Fall? NFL TV: Fox Network? CBS?

Games? Skating exhibitions?

This what? Arrangements, competitions?

CBS? Olympics?

Games? Figure-skating competitions?

PREVENTIVE ACTION

How alert you need to be to pronoun-triggered ambiguity in your editing depends in large measure on how careful you are about pronoun-triggered ambiguity when you're *writing*.

There's a simple way to find out if you're being careful *enough*. Get hold of something you have written—but haven't edited—and read through it with only one purpose in mind: to identify all the pronouns and to verify that the pronoun/ referent connection is absolutely clear. To make sure you're not fooling yourself, I suggest the following step: that each time you come across a pronoun, you draw a circle around it (a mental circle is okay). With each circle, ask yourself the following question—"Is the referent *obvious?*"

Don't assume anything. Work your way backwards. Make sure the referent is the most *obvious* candidate, bearing in mind that you, as the writer, already know the true identity of the referent.

Be especially careful when a new sentence starts with the pronoun *this* or *it*—and nothing else, as in the following examples:

As you undoubtedly are aware, inflation is under control, unemployment is at an all-time low, and corporate profits are solid. **This** is good reason to be optimistic about the economy.

Clara Ames has never questioned any of the decisions she has made in her career as a tightrope-walking harpist. **This** is a big factor in her confidence.

In each of the preceding examples, the referent for the pronoun that launches the second sentence is not a specific word, but an idea. And although there is no law against using *this* or *it* to refer to an idea that has been introduced in the previous sentence, the idea needs to be much more obvious than it is in these two examples. You need to ask yourself, "this *what?*" If the answer isn't obvious, clarify.

If, after going through this exercise, you've reassured yourself that the brain of even the laziest of readers isn't likely to make erroneous pronoun/referent connections, you can count yourself fortunate: You have one less thing to worry about when you edit. But don't get too complacent. Pronouns crop up so frequently in writing, and the tendency to assume that their referents are obvious is so great, that even the most careful of editors will sometimes let faulty pronoun/referent connections slip by.

SOLVING THE PROBLEM

You can edit your way out of pronoun/referent problems in one of two ways. The first way is to simply replace the pronoun with either the referent itself, or a synonym. The second is to rewrite the sentence, eliminating the pronoun altogether. Here's a closer look at each option:

Replacing the pronoun with the referent

Nothing fancy here. You simply ditch the pronoun, and replace it with the actual referent or a reasonable facsimile thereof. If you're uncomfortable about having the same word crop up twice in adjacent sentences, you can use a synonym. But don't wear out your thesaurus trying to come up with substitute words. As long as you don't overdo it, repeating the same word in the same paragraph or even in the same sentence isn't nearly as upsetting or disruptive to readers as many writers believe, as the following examples should illustrate:

> The new storage units have become a problem for the managers. ~~They~~ **The managers** simply do not like the fact that ~~they~~ **the units** are being used as trash receptacles.

> The lab workers store the chemicals in a freezer where the temperatures are 30 degrees below zero. ~~They~~ **The chemicals** remain there for six months.

> I asked the doctor to examine the bump on my head. When he looked at my head, he said: "~~It~~ **The bump** has to come off."

> CBS, which lost professional football rights to the Fox network, is expected to program a number of figure-skating competitions against the NFL TV games next fall ~~It~~ **and** is already making preparations for ~~that~~ **these competitions**. ~~This~~ **Televising figure-skating** would be natural for CBS since ~~CBS~~ **it** is showing the Winter Olympic Games beginning Feb. 12 ~~It~~ **and** has already secured rights for **the Winter Olympics** in 1998.

Reworking the sentence

This approach to solidifying the pronoun/referent connection is trickier to pull off than option number one, but it often produces a smoother sentence. In each of the examples below, the ambiguity has been eliminated by changing the fundamental structure of the original sentences.

The store managers do not like the fact that ~~The~~ the new storage units ~~have become a problem for the store managers. They simply do not like the fact that they~~ are now being used as trash receptacles.

The lab workers store the chemicals **for six months** in a freezer where the temperatures are 30 degrees below zero. ~~They remain there in some instances for as long as six months.~~

CBS, which lost professional football rights to the Fox network, is expected to program a number of figure-skating competitions against the NFL TV games next fall. ~~It is already making~~ Preparations for the televising of these competitions **are now under way.**

AND ONE FOR GOOD MEASURE

Here, for good measure, is one last example of how to edit sentences in which the pronoun/referent connection isn't as solid as it needs to be. As you will see, both options described in the preceding section do the job.

ORIGINAL

Many communities have struggled for centuries to preserve local laws and standards, but when they clash with those of the outside world, they experience new problems that defy traditional solutions.

EDITED

Many communities have struggled for centuries to preserve local laws and standards, but when ~~they~~ **these laws and standards** clash with those of the outside world, ~~they~~ **new problems** arise that defy traditional solutions.

8

Put Modifiers in Their Place

Modifiers—words and phrases that either broaden or narrow the meaning of other words in the same sentence—are best looked upon as the chaperones or, better still, the Secret Service agents of language: Unless they are literally glued to the word or phrase they're supposed to modify, they're not doing their jobs. And here's a not-very-pretty picture at what can happen:

> Madeline and Phil spent the evening listening to Whitney Houston sing show tunes with their cat, Maurice.

> Jennifer came to the party with her husband wearing a pink chiffon dress.

> Riddled with fleas, my friend Delbert had no choice: he had to fumigate the house.

Silliness, yes? But easily explained. The position in each of these sentences of the modifying phrases—"with their cat, Maurice," "wearing a pink chiffon dress," and "riddled with fleas"—induces us to attach that phrase to the wrong word. Maurice the cat wasn't singing along with Whitney Houston; he was sitting with Madeline and Phil. It was Jennifer, not her husband, wearing the pink chiffon dress. And it was the house, not Delbert, that was riddled with fleas.

There's a simple enough way to clear up this confusion: You simply reposition the modifiers next to the words they're supposed to modify. Before you can do this, though, you need to be able to recognize when the modifiers aren't where they ought to be. This chapter is designed to sharpen your capacity to do just that.

UNDANGLING "DANGLING" PHRASES

A phrase or clause "dangles" when the idea or image it expresses does not connect logically to the idea or image it is supposed to be modifying. "Dangle," though, is probably not the best word to describe what's actually happening. Dangling phrases don't really dangle. They simply attach themselves to the wrong word, as evidenced by the following examples:

> After having been in the oven for four hours, you are now ready to serve the roast.

> While dialing your number, my car went out of control and almost hit a utility pole.

> Mouth drooling after the novocaine shot, my dentist advised me not to try to sing any opera arias for at least three hours.

In each of the preceding sentences, the phrase that introduces the main clause is creating a misleading picture of who, in fact, has just spent four hours in the oven, who or what was dialing a number on a car phone, and whose mouth was drooling from the novocaine.

You bring order to this confusion in one of two ways, neither of them complicated. The simpler of the two options is to convert the dangling phrase to a clause—a group of words that contains a verb and its subject. The second option is to change the word sequence in the main body of the sentence. Here's a closer look at both options:

Converting the dangling phrase to a clause

This approach to undangling dangling elements consists of replacing the verbal phrase in the introductory phrase with its true verb counterpart, and pairing that verb with its rightful subject. You will notice in the following examples that the presence of both a verb *and* its subject in the clauses that introduce the main thought eliminates the confusion that reigned when the introductory phrase was dominated by the verbal alone. Here, incidentally, is one of the advantages that clauses have over phrases. Because a clause contains both a subject and its verb, the question of *who* is doing to *what* never arises.

> After ~~having been~~ **the roast has been** in the oven for four hours, you are now ready to serve ~~the roast~~ **it.**

> While ~~dialing~~ **I was dialing** your number, my car went out of control and I almost hit a utility pole.

> ~~My mouth drooling~~ **Because my** mouth **was drooling** after the novocaine shot, my dentist advised me not to sing any opera arias for at least three hours.

Shifting word sequence in the main clause

In this option, the dangling element remains untouched. You tinker instead with the wording in the main clause. Your goal: to make sure that the doer of the action expressed in the introductory phrase is the *first* noun or pronoun the reader encounters in the main clause.

Editing the sentence in this way isn't major surgery, by any means, but if you use this option, you should be prepared to make adjustments elsewhere in the sentence. In the first and last of the examples below, for instance, the voice of the verb has been switched from active to passive—an issue we'll look at more closely in Chapter 11.

> After having been in the oven for four hours, ~~you are~~ **the roast** is now ready to ~~serve~~ **be served.** ~~the roast.~~

> While dialing your number, ~~my car went out of~~ **I lost** ~~went out of~~ **control of the car** and almost hit a utility pole.

> Mouth drooling after the novocaine shot, **I was advised** by **my** dentist ~~advised me~~ not to sing any opera arias for the next three hours.

CLEARING UP RELATIVE CONFUSION

Clauses that begin with a relative pronoun (*who, that,* or *which*) can create confusion when more than one noun is lurking in the cluster of words that precedes the pronoun. Here are several sentences that exemplify this problem, followed by the edits that eliminate the ambiguity:

> ORIGINAL
> The songs in the new Hanson album that everyone is talking about are the duets. [What is everyone talking about: the "songs" or the "albums"?]

Edited
The songs ~~in this new Hanson album~~ that everyone
is **talking about in the new Hanson album** are
the duets.

Original
One of the important issues in this trial that few
people have paid attention to is the fact that the
Doberman who allegedly bit the mailman has no
recollection of the incident. [What is it that people
haven't paid much attention to: the trial or the
Doberman's faulty memory?]

Edited
One of the important issues ~~in this trial~~ that few
people have paid attention to **in this trial** is the fact
that the Doberman that allegedly bit the mailman
has no recollection of the incident.

Original
The daughter of the owner, who was never interested
in the movie business, now wants to run the show.
[Which family member wasn't interested?]

Edited
The **owner's** daughter ~~of the owner~~, who was never
interested **herself** in the movie business, now wants
to run the show.

BAD TIMING

Modifying phrases and clauses introduced by adverbs that relate
to time—*after, before, during, when, as*, etc.—warrant extra scrutiny

during editing, especially in sentences that house two clauses, each with its own time frame. In the examples that follow, several types of action are described, but with a good deal of confusion over the timing of the actions.

ORIGINAL

Everyone was surprised when Lucifer got up and announced that he was going to retire immediately after the coffee was served.

EDITED

Everyone was surprised when Lucifer got up **immediately after the coffee was served** and announced that he was going to retire. ~~immediately after the coffee was served.~~

ORIGINAL

I can frequently see pigeons lying in my bed as I look out my bedroom window each morning.

EDITED

As I lie in my bed each morning and look out my bedroom window, I can frequently see pigeons. ~~lying in my bed each morning as I look out my bedroom window.~~

ORIGINAL

When the idea for a line of diamond-studded left-handed tools was first introduced more than 100 years ago, our lawyer informed us that no other company held any patents.

EDITED

~~When the idea~~ **Our lawyer informed us that when the idea** for a line of diamond-studded left-handed tools was first introduced more than 100 years ago, ~~our lawyer informed us that~~ no other company held any patents.

DOUBLE AGENTS

English is saddled with a handful of modifiers that can operate as either adjectives *or* adverbs, and, because of this split personality, are a common source of ambiguity. The most notorious member of this family of modifiers is *only*, although the modifier *both* can be equally troubling. The main problem you face when you deal with these modifiers is that the correct choice, technically speaking, often sounds awkward. Here's a sentence that illustrates the core problem:

Frank and Elise only balked at the price at the last minute.

The problem with this sentence as written is that you can interpret its meaning in several ways:

➤ that Frank and Elise were the *only* couple out of a group of couples that balked at the price at the last minute
➤ that Frank and Elise only *balked* at the price at the last minute, but eventually went along with the deal
➤ that Frank and Elise waited until the last minute before balking at the price

Under normal circumstances, you would clear up the ambiguity found in the examples you've just read by positioning *only* before or after the word it's meant to modify. Doing so, however, can sometimes create an awkward-sounding sentence. If the lyricist who wrote the standard "I Only Have Eyes For You" had adhered to the proximity principle, for instance, the song would have been entitled "I Have Eyes Only For You," or "I Have Eyes For Only You," and, who knows, the song might never have caught on.

So my advice when you come across a sentence with a modifier such as *only* or *both* is to be not only careful, but also flexible. Decide which word in the sentence the modifier should modify; and try to position the modifier as close to that word as possible. If, though, the change produces an awkward rhythm, you might want to rewrite the sentence altogether, as in the following examples:

> Frank and Elise **were the only two people who** ~~only~~ balked at the price at the last minute.

> Frank and Elise ~~only~~ balked at the price at the last minute, **but they eventually went along with the deal.**

> **It wasn't until the last minute that** Frank and Elise ~~only~~ balked at the price. ~~at the last minute.~~

9

Zero in on Subjects
and Their Verbs

O ne of the messier tasks you are sometimes called upon to carry out when you edit either your own work or anybody else's is to simplify and bring order to overstuffed and unwieldy sentences. Let's not worry for now about *why* the sentence was overstuffed and unwieldy to begin with, and let's focus instead on what your first move ought to be when you are confronted with such a sentence. My recommendation is to take what I call the "Who-Do" approach.

"WHO-DO" WRITING AT A GLANCE

The fundamental idea behind the "Who-Do" principle as an editing tool is to take care of the basics before you do anything else. You do this, first of all, by identifying the subject of the sentence (the "who") and then identifying its verb (the "do"), although it is sometimes easier to start with the verb and figure out which word in the sentence is "doing" whatever the verb is doing.

Either way, though, once you have determined which two words or groups of words are filling these roles, your next move should be to check to see whether the "who" and "do" are (1) operating in tandem;

and (2) located at or near the front of the sentence. If not, you should unite them, and, if necessary, move them closer to the front.

Meeting the reader's need for meaning

The rationale behind "Who-Do" editing becomes clear when you take into account the basic dynamics of reading. Reading, remember, is ultimately a search for meaning, and before readers can distill any meaning from a group of words, they must first be able to identify (and connect) both the "who" and the "do" of the thought, and they must usually be able to connect that tandem to the complement—the word or words that join with a subject and verb to form the thought.

It follows, therefore, that the sooner readers can figure out which specific words in a sentence are filling these fundamental roles, the sooner they'll be able to grasp the meaning of the sentence. It also follows that the harder it is and the longer it takes for readers to identify these words, the tougher the sentence becomes to navigate.

To illustrate what happens when the positioning of the "who" and "do" *interferes* with the reader's ability to figure out what the sentence is about, draw in a deep breath and try to work your way through the following sentence, which typifies academic writing at its windiest:

> Reorganizing a school into smaller units, by increasing flexibility for rescheduling students to meet their individual needs and by allowing for back-to-back scheduling of the core academic classes to provide opportunities for an entire team of teachers and students to meet for extended periods of time in in-depth interdisciplinary happenings, results in more creative and profitable use of human potential.

It isn't enough to say that this sentence is too long. Far more troublesome than its length is its structure—that Gobi-like expanse of verbal real estate that separates the "who" of the main thought ("reorganizing") from the "do" of the main thought ("needs").

Look now at an equally long but infinitely more readable sentence written by Lewis Lapham, the editor of *Harper's Magazine.*

> As is the habit of actors, Nixon brooded over the worth and beauty of his image in the press, often peering through the newspapers for two and three hours at a time, and when I listened to Washington reporters talk about his obsessive marking up of their copy, I thought of the mechanical toy reading the label on its box, trying to figure out what it was that the manufacturers had in mind.

Let us not concern ourselves with either the wording or the quality of thought that differentiates the quality of thought in Lapham's sentence from the quality of thought in the "reorganizing the school" sentence. Let's focus instead on the *structure* of each sentence. Lapham's sentence is clearly the more readable of the two; and one reason, at least, is that the sentence adheres to the "Who-Do" principle. The subject and verb of the main thought appear early in each of the sentence's two independent clauses, and they appear early in the dependent clause as well. What's more, the subject and verb operate in tandem in all three instances. Here's a closer look:

> As is the habit of actors, **Nixon** [who] **brooded** [do] over the worth and beauty of his image in the press, often peering through the newspapers for two and three hours at a time, and when **I** [who] **listened** [do] to Washington reporters talk about his obsessive marking up of their copy, **I** [who]

thought [do] of the mechanical toy reading the label on its box, trying to figure out what it was that the manufacturers had in mind.

PUTTING THE CONCEPT TO WORK

Simplistic though it may seem, the "Who-Do" principle is an enormously versatile tool, and it is particularly useful when you come up against sentences as lengthy and as convoluted as the "reorganizing the school" nightmare I threw your way at the beginning of this chapter. Look what happens to the readability of that sentence when we unite the "who" and the "do" of the sentence. Notice, too, how much clearer the writing becomes when we break the original sentence into individual sentences, each with its own "who" and "do" operating in tandem and appearing early in each sentence.

> **Reorganizing the school into smaller units** [who] **results** [do] in a far more creative and profitable use of human potential. **It** [who] **increases** [do] ~~By its increasing~~ flexibility, **for it** [who] **now becomes** [do] **possible to** ~~for rescheduling making it possible~~ set up schedules that meet the individual needs of students.
>
> **It** [who] **also allows** [do] for back-to-back scheduling of the core academic classes and thus **provides** [do] opportunities for an entire team of teachers and students to meet for extended periods of time in in-depth interdisciplinary happenings. ~~results in a more creative and profitable use of human potential.~~

This passage could still benefit from some pruning. If nothing else, though, we've stopped the bleeding. Readers can figure out the meaning without having to hack their way through a jungle of verbiage.

Avoiding the "Dick and Jane" Effect

The simplicity of the "Who-Do" concept might lead you to believe that if you rely too heavily on this pattern in your sentences, your writing will sound as if it belongs in a grade-school reading primer.

That concern is understandable. It is also unwarranted. To prove my point, consider the following two paragraphs, each of them the product of a writer—John Leonard in the first instance, and Gary Wills in the second instance—who is widely admired for his stylish prose. You'll notice that throughout these paragraphs the subject and verb of the main thought operate in tandem and appear early on in the sentence. Yet, you could hardly call the style of either paragraph simplistic or monotonous. Each writer has dodged this bullet in two ways: first, by varying the length of the sentences; and, second, by varying the rhythm of the sentences with deftly placed interior phrases.

JOHN LEONARD

Anyway, the flu epidemic hit our house over the holiday weekend. It looks as though it intends to stay for the entire year of the Monkey. We had intended to participate in the New York Road Runners Club seven-mile reversible scoot in Central Park, and then to renovate a brownstone, and then to free the hostages in Teheran, and finally to solve the transportation muck-up at Lake Placid. We stayed home instead in tubs of phlegm. After I had finished explaining George Bush, there was nothing left to discuss. I consulted the television listings.

There, at five o'clock on a Sunday afternoon, was Casablanca. I asked the children if they wanted to see Casablanca. I was informed by the children that they had never seen Casablanca at all.

A CLOSER LOOK
Anyway, the flu **epidemic** [who] **hit** [do] our house over the holiday weekend. It [who] **looks** [do] as though it [who] **intends** [do] to stay for the entire year of the Monkey. We [who] **had intended** [do] to participate in the New York Road Runners Club seven-mile reversible scoot in Central Park, and then to renovate a brownstone, and then to free the hostages in Teheran, and finally to solve the transportation muck-up at Lake Placid. We [who] **stayed** [do] home instead in tubs of phlegm. After I [who] **had finished** [do] explaining George Bush, there was nothing left to discuss. I [who] **consulted** [do] the television listings. There [who], at five o'clock on a Sunday afternoon, **was** [do] Casablanca. I [who] **asked** [do] the children if they wanted to see Casablanca. I [who] **was informed** [do] by the children that they had never seen Casablanca at all.

GARY WILLS
Plato clearly meant for us to see Socrates in an agonistic context. His man has a relish for the fray, and he plays rough. When Socrates stretches the rules, his admirers claim he is just satirizing the sophists' methods. But it is his method to demand that others respond briefly and say only what they truly believe, while he engages in long and hypothetical arguments. He takes up role-playing, saying for instance that he wants to take lessons

in defeating the person he will impersonate. He accuses others of cheating, and is accused in return.

A CLOSER LOOK

Plato [who] clearly **meant** [do] for us to see Socrates in an agonistic context. His **man** [who] **has** [do] a relish for the fray, and **he** [who] **plays** [do] rough. When Socrates stretches the rules, his **admirers** [who] **claim** [do] he is just satirizing the sophists' methods. But **it** [who] **is** [do] his method to demand that others respond briefly and say only what they truly believe, while **he** [who] **engages** [do] in long and hypothetical arguments. **He** [who] **takes up** [do] role-playing, saying for instance that he wants to take lessons in defeating the person he will impersonate. **He** [who] **accuses** [do] others of cheating, and **is accused** [do] in return.

A FINAL LOOK

Now that you understand the basic idea of "Who-Do" writing, let us put the concept to work in one last sentence. It comes from a consultant's report that was, in fact, filled with sentences as awkwardly structured as the sentence that follows:

> High-tech businesses that hope to maintain their competitive edge and continue their growth in today's era of intense competition, price-sensitive market pressures, and uncertain conditions abroad that could destabilize international markets need a diversification strategy.

This sentence contains all the requisite parts: subject, verb, and complement. In terms of sentence geography, though, the two key parts of this trio—the subject and the verb—are in separate zip codes.

There's a term to describe sentences in which subjects and their verbs are deliberately separated or purposely positioned near the end of the sentence. They're called periodic sentences, and if you construct such a sentence carefully, it can build suspense. As such, it can be a valuable device in fiction and in humor. I doubt, though, that the writer's aim in this sentence was to create suspense, or to amuse.

In the first of the two edited versions that follow, the information is now communicated in two separate sentences, each with its own "who" and "do." The second version qualifies roughly as a periodic sentence, although you'll notice that the subject and the verb are operating in tandem.

> **In today's marketplace,** high-tech businesses ~~that hope to maintain their competitive edge and continue their growth in today's era~~ **need a diversification strategy. Otherwise, they will not be able to maintain their growth in the face** of intense competition, price-sensitive market pressures, and uncertain conditions abroad that could destabilize international markets need a diversification strategy.

Or:

> **If** high-tech businesses ~~that~~ hope to maintain their growth in the upcoming era of intense competition, price-sensitive market pressures, and uncertain conditions abroad that threaten to destabilize

international markets, **they** need a diversification strategy.

To repeat the drill: Whenever you come across a long and unwieldy sentence, zero in on the main subject and its verb, and check to see whether these two fundamental sentence parts are acting in tandem and are located at or near the beginning of the sentence. If they're not, recast the sentence according to the "Who-Do" principle. More often than not, the editing needed to set things straight in the rest of the sentence will pretty much take care of itself.

10

Get the Most Out of Verbs

If I come back in my next life as a part of speech, I hope to heaven I'm a verb. It's not that I harbor any prejudices against nouns or adjectives or conjunctions or any of the other parts of speech. It's simply that verbs are to language what Michael Jordan is to basketball, what Armani is to double-breasted suits, and what B. B. King is to the blues. Verbs are the heavy hitters of language—the only part of speech autonomous enough to constitute a sentence unto itself, as in "Stop!" or "Wait!" If the parts of speech were a corporation, the CEO and most of the board members would be verbs. If Madonna decided to strike up an affair with a part of speech, no contest: a verb. "Verbs," writes Donald Hall, "make writing go, and they matter more to our language than any other part of speech."

But there are verbs, and there are verbs, which is to say that even in the rarefied world of verbs, there's a pecking order—verbs that are considered "weak," and verbs that are "strong." Most of the verbs considered "weak" belong to that branch of the verb clan known as "linking" or—you should excuse the expression—"copulative" verbs. And most of these verbs are kin to the most common verb of all, *to be*.

It's not without reason that linking verbs are considered "weak." Sad to say, they can't hack it on their own: If you want to use them

76

to express an idea, you usually have to hook them up to an adjective or a noun. "Strong" verbs need no such help. Some examples:

"Weak"	"Strong"
I **am** the owner of	I **own**
He **was** the driver	He **drove**
She **is** the recipient of	She **has received**
They **were** the cause of	They **caused**

In light of this difference, virtually every how-to writing book advises you to express your ideas with the "strongest" verb possible, and, in particular, to avoid starting your sentences with "It is" or "There are." Instead of writing, "There are many ways you can get to Maine," for example, you write, "You can get to Maine in many ways." Instead of writing, "It was tiring for me to travel to Maine." "The trip to Maine tired me out."

I'm not sure why, but I am not as troubled by "It is" and "There is" constructions as other people who teach writing— just as long as you don't use these constructions in every other sentence. Otherwise, though, I can't quarrel with the notion that, given a choice between a strong verb and a linking verb-plus-noun-or-adjective counterpart, the strong verb is usually the better way to go. Reading the following two paragraphs should show you why. The first version replicates the paragraph as it originally appeared in *The Pillars of Hercules,* by Paul Theroux. In the doctored version, I have deliberately replaced the action verb with a phrase that uses a form of the verb *to be,* followed by an adjective or noun.

ORIGINAL
Sentiments of this sort in Dali's autobiography shocked George Orwell, who regarded him as abnormal, without any morality, and James Thurber, who jeered at him. Dali simply laughed:

his book had succeeded in upsetting readers. He spent his life attempting to outrage people's sense of decency; he played at perversion and then came to believe in it, even in the nonsense he uttered. In his eyes there was no portrait or landscape that could not be improved by adding another breast, or a corpse, or a handful of ants.

DOCTORED
Sentiments of this sort in Dali's autobiography were a shock to George Orwell, whose opinion of Dali was that he was abnormal, without any morality, and James Thurber, who had a jeering attitude toward him. Dali simply was amused: his book was successful in upsetting readers. His life was a succession of events the goal of which was to be an outrage to people's sense of decency; he was a player at perversion and then became someone who was a believer in it, even in the nonsense that were his utterances. In his eyes there was no portrait or landscape in which there was not a possibility of improvement through the addition of another breast or a corpse, or a handful of ants.

UN-CLOSETING "CLOSET VERBS"

As you may have noticed in the doctored version of the preceding paragraphs, many of the nouns or adjectives in the linking verb constructions are either identical to or bear a suspicious resemblance to action verbs:

DOCTORED	ORIGINAL
were a shock to	**shocked**

was successful at	**had succeeded in**
was a player at perversion	**played at perversion**
were his utterances	**uttered**

Grammarians have a term for noun and adjective phrases that express an idea that could be more succinctly expressed by a true verb. The term is nominalization. I prefer the term "closet verb." "Closet" tells you what you should be doing with these constructions: taking the verb out of the noun or adjective closet, converting it to a pure verb, and then rewriting the sentence to accommodate the change.

Here are some common examples of closet verbs and the verbs that emerge when you "un-closet" them:

CLOSET VERB	PURE VERB
make an appearance	**appear**
engaged in a discussion	**discussed**
is an example of	**exemplifies**
provide with the information	**inform**
make a recommendation	**recommend**
is an illustration of	**illustrates**

Mind you, there's nothing grammatically wrong with closet verbs. They're simply cumbersome and stilted. You will see what I mean when you compare the following sets of sentences. The first sentence in each set is built around a closet verb. In the edited version, the verb has been taken out of the closet.

ORIGINAL
A successful conclusion to the negotiations is likely to result in a diminution or disappearance of the military presence in the region.

EDITED

~~A successful conclusion to~~ **If the** negotiations **conclude successfully,** ~~is likely to result in a diminution or disappearance of~~ the military presence in the region **should diminish or disappear.**

ORIGINAL

It was Dr. Fogel's belief that taking into account the relation between words and facts is the essential need of a theory of meaning.

EDITED

~~It was~~ Dr. Fogel~~'s belief~~ **believed that a theory of meaning needs to take** ~~taking~~ into account the relation between words and facts. ~~is the essential need of a theory of Meaning.~~

ORIGINAL

These results are a signal that Fly By Night Inc. is making a move in the right direction.

EDITED

These results ~~are a signal~~ **signify** that Fly By Night Inc. is ~~making a move~~ **moving** in the right direction.

ORIGINAL

If we had been given the information earlier about Nero's wishes, we would have made the recommendation that the purchase of the violin take place immediately.

EDITED

If we had been ~~given the information earlier~~ **informed earlier** about Nero's wishes, we would have ~~made a recommendation that the purchase of a violin take place immediately.~~ **recommended that the violin be purchased immediately.**

HALFWAY MEASURES

You don't have to take closet verbs *entirely* out of the closet to enhance the readability of the sentences in which you detect these cumbersome constructions. You can also convert the closet verb to an infinitive (the root form of the verb preceded by *to*) or a gerund (a noun formed by adding *ing* to a root of the verb). The choice between the two should generally come down to which form sounds more natural. Some examples:

ORIGINAL
Eastwood's agent hopes to **bring the contract talks to a conclusion** by early next week.

INFINITIVE
Eastwood's agent hopes to ~~bring the negotiations to a conclusion~~ **conclude the contract talks** by early next week.

CLOSET VERB
The Barnes Group is interested **in the acquisition of** a professional nudist volleyball team.

GERUND
The Barnes Group is interested **in acquiring** a professional nudist volleyball team.

CLOSET VERB
The reorganization of the financial structure of our moat maintenance business was one of our

major achievements last year and marked **the achievement of** a goal that we worked exceptionally hard to meet.

GERUND AND INFINITIVE

~~The reorganization of~~ **Reorganizing** the financial structure of our moat maintenance business was one of our major achievements last year and ~~marked the achievement of~~ **enabled us to achieve** a goal that we worked exceptionally hard to meet.

A FINAL LOOK

To further illustrate how much tighter and zippier sentences become when you fuel them with strong verbs, consider the following two versions of the same paragraph, which comes from an essay by Annie Dillard. You will notice in the original version of the paragraph that almost every sentence is powered by a strong verb. In the doctored version, I have deliberately substituted these strong verbs with either a closet verb construction or a linking verb followed by an adjective or noun. You can judge the impact for yourself, and you can then read through the final paragraph of the set and see how the changes work on a line-by-line basis.

ORIGINAL

We judge a work on its integrity. Often we examine integrity by asking what it makes for itself and what it attempts to borrow from the world. Sentimental art attempts to force persistent emotions upon us. Instead of creating characters and events which will elicit feelings unique to the event, sentimental art gestures toward stock characters and events whose accompanying emotions come on tap.

DOCTORED VERSION

We make a judgment of a work based on its integrity. Often we make an examination of integrity by posing a question of what it makes for itself and what its attempts are to borrow from the world. Sentimental art makes an attempt to impose the force of persistent emotions on us. Instead of effecting the creation of characters and events which will bring about the elicitation of feelings unique to the event, sentimental art makes gestures toward stock characters and events whose accompanying emotions come on tap.

AN INSIDE LOOK

We ~~make a judgment of~~ **judge** a work based on its integrity. Often we ~~make an examination of~~ **examine** integrity ~~by posing a question of~~ **by asking** what it makes for itself and what ~~its attempts are~~ **it attempts** to borrow from the world. Sentimental art ~~makes an attempt~~ **attempts** to ~~impose the force of~~ **force** persistent emotions on us. Instead of ~~effecting the creation of~~ **creating** characters and events which will ~~bring about the elicitation of~~ **elicit** feelings unique to the event, sentimental art ~~makes gestures~~ **gestures** toward stock characters and events whose accompanying emotions come on tap.

11

Make Sure Your Voice is in Good Shape

One of the things you are frequently told *not* to do when you write is something I'm doing in this sentence, which is to express a verb in the passive voice. I'll get to why you're frequently told not to express verbs in the passive voice (as opposed to the active voice) in a moment, after which I'll point out why it sometimes makes good editing sense to ignore this advice. First, though, some definitions.

Contrary to what their names imply, the difference between the active and passive voice of verbs has nothing to do with how much action is embedded in the meaning of the verb itself. Testosterone-packed, Chuck Norris–type verbs, like *stomp, shoot, destroy,* and *annihilate,* can be expressed as easily in one voice as in the other—and without incurring the wrath of your neighborhood grammar cop. Same goes for sedentary, slippers-by-the-fire-type verbs like *read, consider,* and *suggest.*

What, then, is the difference? It's mainly how the structure of the sentence is affected. In sentences or clauses built around verbs in the active voice, the "doer" of the action is always the subject of the sentence or clause, and the verb is followed by the direct object, as in the following examples:

William Shakespeare [doer] **wrote** [verb in the active voice] **Macbeth** [direct object] in the early 1600s.

Lady Macbeth [doer] **delivers** [verb in the active voice] her famous "out damned spot" **speech** [direct object] in the final act.

The scenario changes when the verb is expressed in the passive voice. The direct object of the verb moves up in the world: It becomes the subject of the sentence. And the verb's true subject either disappears or takes on a less conspicuous role—usually the object of the preposition *by*. The form of the verb changes, too. Verbs in the passive voice are always preceded by a form of the verb *to be*, and are always expressed in the past participle form of the verb, as in:

Macbeth [subject of sentence but not the doer of the action] **was written** [verb in the passive voice] by **William Shakespeare** [doer of action is now the object of preposition "by"] in the early 1600s.

The famous "Out damned spot" **speech** [direct object expressed as subject of sentence] **is delivered** [verb in the passive voice] by **Lady Macbeth** [doer of action is now the object of preposition "by"] in the final act.

Or:

The famous "Out, damned spot" speech **is delivered** in the final act. [The doer of the action isn't named.]

As you can see from these examples, the verb's voice has no impact on the *meaning* of the sentence. So the logical question is, why choose one instead of the other? One reason is emphasis. In passive voice constructions, the "doer" gets less attention than the action that was done. The more obvious reason, though, is the tone and feel of the sentence. Sentences with verbs in the active voice tend to flow more smoothly and to sound less formal and bureaucratic than sentences built around verbs in the passive voice— and for a logical reason. The word sequence produced by verbs in the active voice—subject, verb, direct object—mirrors the way we normally speak. Clark Gable, in *Gone With the Wind*, did not say, "Frankly, Scarlett, a damn isn't given by me," and Humphrey Bogart, in *Casablanca*, didn't say, "It should be played again, Sam." Consider, too, the impact the passive voice would have had on the memorability of the following quotes.

"The Alamo should be remembered."

"A book cannot be told by its cover."

"Go ahead, my day will be made by you."

"The torpedoes should be damned."

"The broth can be spoiled by too many cooks."

"The worm is gotten by the early bird."

IN DEFENSE OF THE PASSIVE VOICE

It's easy to beat up on the passive voice. It *is* clunky. It *is* impersonal. And sentences built around passive voice constructions can indeed sound stilted and legalistic.

But let's get carried away.

For one thing, you don't always have a choice. In certain organizations or in certain forms of writing—legal, financial, and scientific, for instance—it is standard procedure to either de-emphasize or conceal the identity of the "doer" in the sentence, as in the following examples:

> Mistakes were made. [Nobody wants to mention who made them.]

> When the icon appears, it should be dragged to the side of the screen. [It doesn't matter who drags it.]

Sometimes, too—more often, certainly, than the grammar checker on your word processor might lead you to believe—the passive voice is actually a *better* choice for you, even when you're under no obligation to use it.

A case in point is the following paragraph, taken from *The Joy of Books* by Eric Burns, who cares as much about careful writing as anyone I know. As you will see, every sentence in this paragraph is built around a verb in the passive voice. But this is not because Burns didn't know any better, or that his grammar checker was asleep at the switch. He uses the passive voice because he wants the spotlight in each of the sentences to shine upon the action that was taken, and not who did it. And the paragraph reads fine, thank you—much smoother, I submit, than would have been the case had Burns slavishly gone along with conventional active voice dogma.

> As Originally Written
> The information was set down on pages that had started out in life as handfuls of clay, gathered at riverbanks and formed into tablets. While still moist, the tablets were poked with sticks and pushed with fingertips, the primitive equivalent of printing. Then they were placed on beds of grass

and left to dry in the sun, sometimes overnight, sometimes for several days, the heat making the language indelible.

Finally, the tablets were bound together with snaps of leather or reed, and the result, loosely speaking, was a book—baked, not published.

DOCTORED (ALL ACTIVE VOICE)
Whoever did the writing set down the information on pages that had started out in life as handfuls of clay, and that other people had gathered at riverbanks and had formed into tablets. These people poked the tablets while still moist with sticks and pushed the tablets with fingertips, the primitive equivalent of print. Someone then placed tablets on beds of grass and left them to dry in the sun, sometimes overnight, sometimes for several days, the heat making the language indelible. Finally, somebody bound the tablets together with snaps of leather or reed, and the result, loosely speaking, was a book—baked, not published.

Going with the flow

In some situations, the choice between the active or passive voice will come down to nothing more complicated than how the sentence *sounds*. In each of the sets of examples that follow, the active-voice form of the verb creates either an awkward flow or an awkward juxtaposition of words. Switching voices solves the problem easily.

ACTIVE VOICE
The dyeing and printing process Palais Royal uses produces colors that are bright, colorfast,

and fade-resistant. [Juxtaposition of "uses" and "produces" is awkward.]

PASSIVE VOICE
The dyeing and printing process ~~Palais Royal uses~~ **used by Palais Royal** produces colors that are bright, colorfast, and fade-resistant.

ACTIVE VOICE
Most people assume that people who edit spend all of their time red-penciling their way through manuscripts. [Repeating "people" creates momentary confusion.]

PASSIVE VOICE
It's commonly assumed that ~~Most people assume that~~ people who edit spend all of their time red-penciling their way through manuscripts.

ACTIVE VOICE
Several studies lend credence to this theory. A University of California psychologist named Rolf Magee conducted the most widely known of these studies in the early 1950s. [Awkward transition between the two sentences.]

PASSIVE VOICE
Several studies lend credence to this theory. ~~A University of California psychologist named Rolf Magee conducted~~ The most widely known of these studies **was conducted in the early 1950s by a University of California psychologist named Rolf Magee.** ~~the widely known these studies in the early 1950s.~~

89

ACTIVE VOICE
Mr. Buchanan's supporters gleefully cheered his characterization of George Will as a yapping "poodle" who deserved a few swats with a rolled-up newspaper. A press corps that thinks Mr. Will and his employer, ABC News, has been too quiet about the fact that Mr. Will's wife who works for the Dole campaign also admired this characterization.

PASSIVE VOICE
Mr. Buchanan's characterization of George Will as a yapping "poodle" who deserved a few swats with a rolled-up newspaper **was gleefully cheered** by his supporters. **It was also admired** by a press corps that thinks Mr. Will and his employer, ABC News, have been too quiet about the fact that Mr. Will's wife works for the Dole campaign.

12

Cut What You Don't Need, but Don't Go Overboard

"I f it is possible to cut a word out," George Orwell advises us in his famous essay "Politics and the English Language," "always cut it out."

On the face of it, you couldn't ask for better editing advice, especially when it comes to memos, technical reports, and other documents that people do not normally take home to read by the fire or curl up in bed with. Most people today have scarcely enough time to keep up with the reading they do by choice. The last thing they need in the reading they do out of necessity are words that do nothing but take up space on the page.

But let us not carry a sound idea to masochistic extremes. Squeeze any piece of writing hard enough and you can probably find words that you can *possibly* cut. Why limit a haiku verse to *seventeen* syllables? Couldn't you say the same thing in *fifteen* or *sixteen* syllables?

So, as much as I endorse Orwell's advice, I feel obliged to temper it just a bit. By all means, do your best when you edit to eliminate words that aren't pulling their weight; but try to execute this vital aspect of editing in a disciplined, intelligent manner. Make sure that what's left over after you've done your slicing reads clearly, and still maintains the tone you want to convey. Remember, too, that whenever you eliminate words from a sentence you invariably change the rhythm of not only the sentence but of the paragraph as well.

In short, keep your scalpel poised and sharp when you edit, but wield it judiciously, with restraint, and with a sense of purpose. Concentrate mainly on the excess verbiage that falls into the categories we'll be looking at in this chapter.

REDUNDANCIES: WHEN MORE IS LESS

Redundancies are words or groups of words that are—well, redundant. They convey information that's already being conveyed by other words and phrases in the same sentence or paragraph. Here's a paragraph excessively overflowing (to get you into the redundancy spirit) with such words and phrases:

> Here are the true facts. My dear, close personal friend Miriam has been a non-paid volunteer for Friends of Maligned Felines for the past three months, and during this period of time has been the chairperson heading the large-sized committee that is responsible for the advance planning of the organization's annual banquet. Miriam has personally herself handwritten the invitations being sent to guests and has met personally face-to-face or spoken personally by phone with each and every member of the organization. True, I will honestly and frankly admit that she has occasionally angered and alienated some of the committee members with whom she serves with her blunt candor, her impatient-type personality, and with her refusal to delegate tasks that she should be assigning to other people in the organization. The end result, however,

is that there will be more members who will be attending this year's banquet than ever before in our history.

Most of the redundancies that bloat the preceding paragraph are obvious—obvious, that is, when you are alert to them. What is a close friend, if not dear or personal? Facts are, by definition, true. Volunteering, last time I checked, is a non-paid activity. And when was the last time a result occurred at either the beginning or middle or a project, as opposed to the end? So you don't need to be a purebred editorial bloodhound, in other words, to keep your writing reasonably free of the most obvious redundancies. You simply need to pay attention. Here's another look at the same paragraph, but this time with the redundancies weeded out:

> Here are the ~~true~~ facts. My ~~dear~~ close ~~personal~~ friend Miriam has been a ~~non-paid~~ volunteer for Friends of Maligned Felines for the past three months, and during this ~~period of~~ time ~~has been the chairperson heading the for~~ has **chaired** the large ~~sized~~ committee responsible for ~~the advance~~ planning ~~of~~ the ~~organization's~~ annual banquet. She has ~~personally~~ handwritten the invitations ~~being sent to guests~~ and has met personally ~~face-to-face~~ or spoken ~~personally~~ by phone with ~~each and~~ every member. ~~of the organization~~ True, ~~I will honestly and frankly admit and confess that~~ she has angered ~~and alienated~~ some ~~of the~~ committee members ~~with whom she serves~~ with her ~~blunt~~ candor, ~~with~~ her ~~impatient-type personality~~ impatience, and ~~with~~ her refusal to delegate. ~~tasks that she should be assigning to other people in the organization But~~ The ~~end~~ result, ~~of her efforts~~ however, is that ~~there~~

~~will be~~ more members ~~who~~ will be attending this
year's banquet than ever before ~~in our history~~.

Categorizing redundancies

A good way to sharpen your ability to spot redundancies is to
familiarize yourself with the various *categories* of redundancies (Oops,
I almost wrote, "The various categories into which redundancies
can be grouped.") Two such categories deserve special mention: (1)
meaningless modifiers, and (2) unnecessary prepositional phrases.
As you peruse the lists that follow, ask yourself how often these
unnecessary words crop up in your writing. Then think about all
the paper we could save if everybody who used these unnecessary
words would suddenly stop doing so.

Meaningless modifiers. A modifier is meaningless when the
attribute it communicates is implicit in the word it modifies. The
list that follows includes several subcategories of these redundancies,
based on the part of speech that is creating the redundancy.

REDUNDANT ADVERBS

~~completely~~ surround   trudge ~~slowly~~
limp ~~awkwardly~~   whisper ~~softly~~
scream ~~loudly~~   ~~angrily~~ berate
fidget ~~nervously~~   mix ~~together~~
pound ~~heavily~~   ~~angrily~~ denounce
~~casually~~ relax   tread ~~lightly~~
scrutinized ~~carefully~~   ~~totally~~ eliminated

REDUNDANT ADJECTIVES

~~free~~ gift   ~~personal~~ opinion
musician ~~by trade~~   ~~required~~ need
~~proposed~~ plan   ~~total~~ extinction

~~tiny~~ speck	a trio ~~of three~~
~~usual~~ habit	~~viable~~ alternative
~~two~~ twins	~~final~~ conclusion
~~firm~~ commitment	~~final~~ ultimatum
~~tail~~ end	~~thrilling~~ excitement
~~trusted~~ advisor	~~shrewd~~ manipulator
~~lively~~ repartee	~~serious~~ crisis
~~horrible~~ disaster	~~odd~~ coincidence
~~light~~ drizzle	~~puzzling~~ quandary

MODIFIERS WITH REDUNDANT MODIFIERS

~~golden~~ blonde	~~most~~ unique
~~emotionally~~ temperamental	~~dark~~ black
~~loyally~~ patriotic	~~excitedly~~ enthusiastic

I could list hundreds of word combinations in which one of the words is simply echoing the meaning of the other. But that in itself would be redundant since the lesson in all these words is the same. If you're going to use modifiers, make sure the modifiers *modify*.

Redundant prepositional phrases. Phrases that begin with a noun followed by the preposition *of* become redundant when the word that follows *of* is an obvious example of the word that precedes *of*. Here's a look at some of these phrases, followed by a paragraph that illustrates why you don't need them.

the city of	the field of
the game of	the language of
the problem of	the nature of
the process of	the period of

REDUNDANT

I was born and went to college in the city of St. Louis. I majored in the field of animal husbandry and also became interested in the game of field hockey, where I played the position of goalie. During this period of time, I became familiar with how universities deal with the problem of underfunding. The nature of this problem is familiar to anybody who goes through the process of raising funds for his or her college.

EDITED

I was born and went to college in ~~the city of~~ St. Louis. I majored in ~~the field of~~ animal husbandry and also became interested in ~~the game of~~ field hockey, where I played ~~the position of~~ goalie. During this ~~period of~~ time, I became familiar with how universities deal with ~~the problem of~~ underfunding. ~~The nature of~~ This problem is familiar to anybody who ~~goes through the process of trying to~~ raises funds for his or her college.

COMPRESSING CUMBERSOME PHRASES

Where to start?

Our everyday language is rife with phrases that communicate in three, four, or even more words, ideas and images that could just as easily be expressed in one or two words. The problem is that most of these phrases have become so ingrained in the vernacular that most people have no idea of how windy they're being when they use these phrases. The list that follows will give you a rough idea of the phrases I'm talking about, and the one or two-word alternates.

after a period of time	**then**
at such time	**when**
at the present time	**now**
due to the fact that	**because**
has the ability to	**can**
have the opportunity	**can** or **is able**
in light of the fact that	**because**
in the event that	**if** or **should**
in the not-too-distant future	**soon**
in view of the fact that	**since**
is in a position to	**can** or **are able**
the way in which	**how**
notwithstanding the fact that	**although**
has the appearance of	**looks like**

Here now is a paragraph infested with such phrases, followed by an edited version:

ORIGINAL

Notwithstanding the fact that we have a concern with respect to the problems that have the potential to arise in the event we proceed with this project, we are now in a position to envision the way in which our two companies might work in concert with one another. We make this statement with confidence due to the fact that we have engaged in lengthy discussions with our advisors, and we are all of the belief that it is important to everyone that we move ahead with as much dispatch as possible.

EDITED

~~Notwithstanding the fact that~~ **Although** we ~~have a~~
~~great concern with respect to~~ **are greatly concerned**
about the problems that ~~have the potential to~~ **might**
arise ~~in the event~~ **if** we proceed with this project,
we ~~are now in a position to~~ **can now** envision ~~the~~
~~way in which~~ **how** our two companies might work
~~in concert with one another~~ **together.** We ~~make this~~
~~statement~~ **say** this with confidence ~~due to the fact~~
~~that~~ **because** ~~we have engaged in lengthy discussions~~
~~with our advisors~~ **we have discussed this topic at**
length and we ~~are~~ all ~~of the belief~~ **believe** ~~that it is~~
~~important to everyone that~~ we **should** move ahead
~~with as much dispatch~~ as **quickly as** possible.

TRIMMING DOWN WORDY CLAUSES

Information expressed in lengthy clauses can often be expressed
in a word or phrase—and without compromising either clarity or
impact. Here are a handful of examples in which wordy clauses have
been converted to phrases or a single word.

ORIGINAL
Although Henderson is not a person normally known
for his diplomatic behavior, he was nonetheless a
model of decorum at last night's meeting.

EDITED
~~Although Henderson is not a person known for his~~
~~diplomatic behavior~~ **Not normally known for his**
diplomacy, Henderson was nonetheless a model of
decorum at last night's meeting.

ORIGINAL

In order to provide you with a convenient way of receiving this information, we will be offering daily updates on our Web site.

EDITED

~~In order to provide you with a convenient way of receiving this information,~~ **For your convenience,** we will be offering daily updates on our Web site.

ORIGINAL

Many of the decisions you need to make when you edit call for a thorough knowledge of punctuation.

EDITED

Many ~~of the decisions you need to make when you edit~~ **editing decisions** call for a thorough knowledge of punctuation.

ORIGINAL

Despite the fact that I have a background in animal husbandry, I have never been able to get my own dogs to fetch.

EDITED

Despite ~~the fact that I I have a background in animal husbandry~~ **my animal husbandry background,** I've never been able to get my own dogs to fetch.

ORIGINAL

We never want to lose sight of the objectives we want to accomplish.

EDITED

We never want to lose sight of ~~the~~ **our** objectives.~~-~~
~~we want to accomplish.~~

A FINAL LOOK

If nothing else, I hope this chapter has convinced you that verbosity (*true* verbosity) in its subtler forms can be exceptionally difficult to spot. This last example should help to dramatize how easily excess verbiage can sneak by you. The original paragraph doesn't *seem* excessively wordy. But as you'll see in the edited version, there's plenty of room to cut—and without scraping bone. You have to know where to look.

ORIGINAL

No matter how extensive our knowledge is about something, the fact that we see it repeatedly has the effect of intensifying the impact it has upon us. An example of this principle in action is Lester Nixon, who is a world-renown trainer of performing fleas. Lester always carries around with him a small brown envelope that has a list of little notes that remind him of all the various things he has to keep in mind when he conducts his daily training sessions.

EDITED

No matter how ~~extensive our knowledge is~~ **extensively we know** ~~about~~ **something,** ~~the fact that we see~~ **seeing** it repeatedly ~~has the effect of intensifying~~ **intensifies** ~~the impact it has upon us~~ **its impact.** ~~An example of this principle in action~~ ~~is~~ **World-renown performing-flea trainer** Lester Nixon, **for example,** ~~who is a world-renown trainer~~

of ~~performing fleas.~~ ~~Lester~~ always carries ~~around~~ ~~with him~~ a small brown envelope that ~~has a list of~~ ~~little notes that remind him~~ of **lists** ~~all the various~~ ~~things~~ **everything** he has to keep in mind when he conducts his daily training sessions.

13

Use Sentence Structure to Control Emphasis

You don't need an advanced degree in linguistics to figure out why information that comes packaged in short, simply constructed sentences is easier for readers to deal with than information packaged in long, more complex sentences.

But there's only one problem: Bare-bones sentences consisting of nothing more than a subject, its verb, and a complement are not versatile enough to accommodate the complexity and texture of the information and ideas that most of us need to get across in our day-to-day writing. Most ideas come with extra baggage—bits of information that expand, clarify, or give added shading to the main idea, and yet are not important enough in their own right to warrant their own sentences. You can't simply slap these bits and pieces of information into your sentences as if you were shoving a pile of junk from your night table into your sock drawer. You need to make sure that the grammatical form you're using to express an idea or an image is the form best suited to the degree of importance you want your readers to attach to each idea or image.

Here's the core principle: Certain types of grammatical forms— that is, certain patterns of word groupings—are better suited than other forms to convey ideas and images that are of *primary* importance to the main idea you're trying to get across; and other structures are better suited to conveying ideas that are of secondary importance. You may already be adhering to this principle intuitively when you write and when you edit. Then again, maybe not. You'll find out soon enough.

EMPHASIS AND STRUCTURE: THE BASICS

To set the stage for the concepts we're going to be dealing with in this chapter, here are five sentences that either express exclusively or include, along with other ideas, the same piece of information: the fact that a particular restaurant—we'll call it Lil's—is extremely noisy.

> ➤ Lil's is an extremely noisy restaurant.
> ➤ Lil's is an extremely noisy restaurant, but the food is great.
> ➤ Although the food is great, Lil's is an extremely noisy restaurant.
> ➤ Although Lil's is an extremely noisy restaurant, the food is great.
> ➤ The food is great at the extremely noisy restaurant named Lil's.

The sentences in the preceding list differ in several respects. But the differences I want to dwell upon relate to the specific grammatical vehicles I have used in each sentence to tell readers that Lil's is one noisy place. These vehicles range from a sentence unto itself (the first of the sentences in the list) to a modifier (the last of the sentences in the list). And I want to draw your attention in particular to how much emphasis each idea gets in each sentence, based on its grammatical uniform.

Here's another look at the list, but this time with an eye toward the specific vehicles that convey the notion that Lil's is a noisy place.

The sequence that follows begins with a sentence in which this idea is given the *most* emphasis. The sequence ends with the sentence in which the idea has been given the *least* emphasis.

> **Lil's is an extremely noisy restaurant.** [*a sentence unto itself*]

> **Lil's is an extremely noisy restaurant,** but the food is great. [*independent clause in a compound sentence*]

> Although the food is great, **Lil's is an extremely noisy restaurant.** [*independent clause in a complex sentence*]

> **Although Lil's is an extremely noisy restaurant,** the food is great. [*dependent clause in a complex sentence*]

> The food is great at the **extremely noisy restaurant** named Lil's. [*modifier and object of preposition*]

The lesson implicit in this sequence should be apparent to you. The *more* emphasis you want to give to an idea or image, the more inclined you should be to express that image or idea as either a simple sentence unto itself or as an independent clause in a compound or complex sentence. The *less* emphasis you want the idea or image to get (relative to other ideas in the sentence) the more inclined you should be to express the idea as either a dependent clause or a modifying phrase.

Let's look now at how you might actually put this principle to work in your editing.

DECIDING WHAT'S IMPORTANT

Before you can determine which grammatical structure is the "best" vehicle for individual ideas or images in a sentence, you need to determine how major a role, relatively speaking, you want those images or ideas to play in the sentence. The following sentence illustrates what happens when you fail to go through this process as a writer, and then fail as an editor to take note of the neglect:

> Pulitzer Prize winner and noted bubble-gum card collector Lydia Snopes, who is a descendant of Edith Wharton, has a beautiful, year-round, easily maintained garden in her lovely, rent-controlled apartment in midtown Manhattan, despite her chronic back problems.

The most obvious problem with this sentence is that it is trying to tell us too much. But it isn't only the *volume* of information that is the problem; it's the way that all the bits and pieces of information have been crowded together. It's tough to decide which aspects of Lydia's life the writer wants to showcase: her bubble-gum card collection, her chronic back problems, her genealogy, her garden, or the fact that she lives in a rent-controlled, midtown Manhattan apartment? This sentence, in short, lacks *shading*. Look at everything it is trying to tell us about Lydia Snopes:

> ➤ She is a Pulitzer Prize winner.
> ➤ She collects bubble-gum cards.
> ➤ She's a descendant of Edith Wharton.
> ➤ She has a beautiful garden that grows year-round.
> ➤ The garden is easy to maintain.
> ➤ She lives in a rent-controlled apartment in midtown Manhattan.
> ➤ The apartment is lovely.
> ➤ She suffers from chronic back problems.

Let's analyze now how the writer has decided to package each of these bits of information.

> **Pulitzer Prize winner** [adjective] and noted bubble-gum card collector [adjective] **Lydia Snopes** [subject], **who is a descendant of Edith Wharton** [subordinate clause], **has** [main verb] a **beautiful** [adjective], **year-round** [adjective], **easily maintained** [adjective] **garden** [complement and direct object] in her **lovely** [adjective], **rent-controlled** [adjective] **apartment** [object of preposition] in **mid-town Manhattan** [object of preposition], despite her chronic back problems [modifying phrase].

You may have noticed in the preceding analysis that the core idea of this sentence—as expressed by the subject, its verb, and the complement—is the fact that Lydia Snopes has a garden. Everything else in the sentence modifies that main idea. Which is okay, except that all these modifying elements are competing so intensely with one another for the reader's attention that they literally cancel one another out.

So let's see if we can give this sentence some badly needed shading. Let's assume, for the sake of argument, that our objective in this particular passage was to emphasize the following point: That despite the fact that she has chronic back problems, Lydia Snopes has managed to create a beautiful year-round garden, the reason being that the garden is easy to maintain.

While the rest of the information—her being a former Pulitzer Prize winner, her bubble-gum card collection, her genealogical link to Edith Wharton, and her rent-controlled apartment in midtown New York—is still interesting and, depending on your audience, somewhat relevant, it is not as crucial. This being the case, the sentence might be edited as follows:

> Former Pulitzer Prize winner ~~and noted bubble-gum-card collector~~ Lydia Snopes ~~who is a descendant of Edith Wharton and~~ **has suffered**

from back problems for years, ~~has a beautiful, year-round, easily maintained garden in her lovely, rent-controlled apartment in midtown Manhattan.~~ **but she has managed nonetheless to create a beautiful year-round garden in her midtown Manhattan apartment. Her secret: The garden is easy to maintain.**

Notice, please, the revised hierarchy of emphasis that now prevails, based on the structures that have been used to convey each idea. The two key ideas in the first sentence— the fact that Lydia has chronic back problems yet still manages to maintain a beautiful gar den—are expressed as independent clauses. And the third key idea—the fact that her garden is easy to maintain—is expressed as a sentence unto itself. Two pieces of information—her bubble-gum card collection and her genealogical link to Edith Wharton— have been dropped altogether (we can add this information in another sentence, if need be), and the rest of the information has been expressed as modifiers.

Let us now assume, for the sake of argument, that you wanted to bump up the importance two aspects of Lydia's background: her Pulitzer Prize and her connection to Edith Wharton. You could accomplish this objective by expressing both ideas as the complement of the opening clause, as in:

~~Former Pulitzer Prize winner and bubble gum collector~~ Lydia Snopes ~~who is a descendent of Edith Wharton~~ **is a Pulitzer Prize winner and a direct descendant of Edith Wharton** ~~has a beautiful, year-round, easily maintained garden in her rent-controlled apartment in midtown Manhattan, despite her chronic back problems~~ **who has had chronic back problems for years. But she has managed nonetheless to create a beautiful,**

Barry Tarshis

> **year-round garden in her midtown Manhattan apartment. Her secret: The garden is very easy to maintain.**

And what if you wanted to highlight Lydia's bubble-gum card hobby? Simple. Change the structure. Convert "bubble-gum collector" from an adjective that modifies Lydia Snopes to the complement of the first clause.

> Former Pulitzer Prize winner ~~and bubble gum collector~~ Lydia Snopes ~~who is a descendent of Edith Wharton~~ **is a noted bubble-gum card collector who is a descendant of Edith Wharton and lives in a lovely rent-controlled apartment in midtown Manhattan. And despite the fact that she has had chronic back problems, she** ~~has a beautiful, year-round, easily maintained garden in her rent-controlled apartment in midtown Manhattan, despite her chronic back problems~~ **has managed to create a beautiful, year-round garden. Her secret: The garden is very easy to maintain.**

WHOSE JOB IS IT, ANYWAY?

I am aware that the edits in the examples we've just looked at come perilously close to that "no-man's-land" that separates "editing" from "rewriting." Strictly speaking, decisions relating to emphasis ought to be made by the writer, not the editor. Remember, though, you're doing double-duty as an editor of your own work. And although there are no formulas you can use to determine how much emphasis you ought to be giving to each individual idea in a sentence—you have to figure it out for yourself on a situation-by-situation basis—I

108

can offer two simple guidelines that will help you immensely once those decisions have been made.

> ➤ Express important ideas in simple sentences or as independent clauses in complex or compound sentences.
> ➤ Be wary of competing modifiers.

Let us take a look now at each of these guidelines, and look, too, at the tools that underlie their application.

MATTERS OF DEPENDENCY

Complex sentences, by definition, always include one clause that is subordinate to the other. That's fine—just as long as the idea expressed in the subordinate clause is indeed the idea you want to de-emphasize. Compare the emphasis in the following two sentences:

Although Tom and Jerry argue constantly, they are the best of friends.

Although Tom and Jerry are good friends, they argue constantly.

The information communicated in each of these sentences is essentially the same, but the structure of the sentences differs, and so does the emphasis. In the first example, the fact that Tom and Jerry argue constantly is expressed as a dependent clause, and the idea of their being good friends is expressed as an independent clause. The result: The emphasis is on the friendship, not the constant arguing. In the second example, the emphasis shifts, and for the same reason: The information in the independent clause gets more emphasis.

At the risk of oversimplifying an issue that is anything but open-and-shut, it is not a bad idea whenever you come across a complex sentence to give it a quick look-see, just to make sure that you consider the information expressed in the dependent clause subordinate to the idea expressed in the independent clause. If this is *not* the case, you have two options: (1) restructure the sentence so that the emphasis gets reversed; or (2) create a compound sentence. Let's look more closely at each option.

Reversing the emphasis

In this option, the two clauses simply trade information. The information in the dependent clause moves to the independent clause, and vice versa. What's nice about this option is that you don't have to fiddle much with the wording. All you have to do is shift the word order.

ORIGINAL
Although Mickey and Minnie seem happy since their move to Orlando, they still have many problems to work through in their relationship.

EDITED
Although Mickey and Minnie ~~seem happy since their move to Orlando, they~~ still have many problems to work through in their relationship, **they seem happy since their move to Orlando.**

ORIGINAL
Despite the fact that we have ironed out many of the minor issues in the contract, we still have a long way to go before we can seal the deal.

EDITED
Despite the fact that we ~~have ironed out many of the minor issues in the contract~~ still have a long way to

go before we can seal the deal, **we have ironed out many of the minor issues in the contract.**

ORIGINAL
Even though she is essentially a loner, Lydia Snopes loves to go ballroom dancing.

EDITED
Even though ~~she is essentially a loner~~ Lydia Snopes loves to go ballroom dancing, **she is essentially a loner.** ~~Lydia Snopes loves to go ballroom dancing~~

Giving each idea equal billing

This is the option to take when you want to give equal emphasis to *both* ideas in complex sentence. Here, too, there isn't much sentence carpentry involved: You simply create a compound sentence.

~~Although~~ Mickey and Minnie seem happy today, **but** they have had many problems in their relationship.

~~Despite the fact that~~ We've ironed out many of the minor issues in the contract, **but** we still have a long way to go before we can seal the deal.

~~Even though~~ Lydia Snopes loves to go ballroom dancing, **but** she is essentially a loner.

KEEPING DEPENDENCY UNDER CONTROL

As I suggested earlier, deciding whether ideas or images ought to be expressed as dependent or independent clauses (or, for that matter, as phrases or modifiers) is always a judgment call, based on how much emphasis you would like each of those ideas or images to get. But there is at least one symptom in writing that almost always signals the need to convert a dependent clause into an independent clause. If the dependent clause is lengthy (more than seven or eight words) or even remotely convoluted, your impulse should be to do one of two things: (1) see if you can cut down on the wording; and (2) if not, think about converting the clause to an independent clause. Think about it. If it is taking you all those words to communicate an idea, the idea *must* be reasonably important. Give it its own stage.

Consider the following sentence:

> Although Mr. Cameron normally disregards what his clients say they want, and instead chooses furnishings and fabrics that reflect his own preferences for early Americana, his regard in this situation for the owners' unselfconscious lifestyle has induced him to broaden the scope of his selections.

You would have a tough time convincing me that it makes any sense at all to cram all the information that comes at the beginning of this sentence into a dependent clause. To prove my point, look at how much easier this sentence is to read once that lengthy and convoluted dependent clause gets converted to an independent clause:

> ~~Although~~ Mr. Cameron normally disregards what his clients say they want, and, instead, chooses furnishings and fabrics that reflect his own preferences for early Americana. **In this situation, however**, his regard ~~in this situation~~ for the owners' unselfconscious lifestyle has induced him to broaden the scope of his selections.

Starting sentences out with wordy, convoluted dependent clauses is an all-too-common tendency in many types of writing, especially in business and academic circles. Fueling the tendency, I think, is an inherent fear among some people that if you express your ideas in simple, declarative sentences, your readers won't take you seriously. Nonsense.

What follows are several examples that illustrate this tendency, and how to deal with it in editing. As you read the original sentences, take note of where in the sentence you find yourself getting bogged down. Chances are, it is well before you have reached the main subject. Note, too, how much clearer and more cogent the writing becomes when the dependent clause is expressed as an independent clause.

ORIGINAL

Although there are passages in this book that demonstrate Mr. Stone's ability to pinpoint the critical factors in various presidential elections throughout the years, such as Harry Truman's whistle-stop tour during the final days of the 1948 campaign and Dwight D. Eisenhower's promise in 1952 that he would go to Korea, the book in general suffers from a lack of focus and a lack of original ideas.

EDITED

~~Although there are passages~~ Mr. Stone demonstrates **in passages throughout** this book ~~that demonstrate Mr. Stone's~~ his ability to pinpoint the critical factors in various presidential elections throughout the years such as Harry Truman's whistle-stop tour during the final days of the 1948 campaign and Dwight D. Eisenhower's promise in 1952 that he would go to Korea. The book in general, **however**, suffers from a lack of focus and a lack of original ideas.

ORIGINAL

In one important set of experiments involving hamsters in which he placed electrodes in a section of the brain known as the lateral nucleus, Carl Bennett noted that the single cells had a spontaneous firing rate.

EDITED

In one important set of experiments involving hamsters ~~in which he placed~~ **Carl Bennett placed** electrodes in a section of the brain known as the lateral nucleus. ~~Carl Bennett.~~ **He then** noted that the single cells had a spontaneous firing rate.

ORIGINAL

Although there has never been a better time than today to take advantage of the combination of low interest rates and high yields on the typical investment portfolio, even if it means taking on more debt, investors should be cautious.

EDITED

~~Although~~ There has never been a better time than today to take advantage of the combination of low interest rates and high yields on the typical investment portfolio—even if it means taking on more debt. **Still and all,** investors should be cautious.

WHEN MODIFIERS COMPETE

Modifiers begin to compete with one another in sentences in in which too *many* words are modified. Here are several sentences that illustrate the problem:

Highly intelligent Morris can occasionally forget his lines during lengthy video tapings.

The brief meeting was highly productive.

The noisy restaurant graciously serves great food.

The readability problem in each of these sentences is that you don't know which idea should get higher billing: Morris's intelligence, or his occasional lapse of memory; how brief the meeting was, or how productive it was; the noise level at the restaurant, its great food, or the gracious service.

Your first response when you come across a sentence in which modifiers appear to be competing with one another should be to step back and decide which of the ideas expressed by the modifiers deserves more emphasis than the others. The next step is to give the more important of those ideas a grammatical form that befits its status. You'll notice in the first of the examples that the basic sentence hasn't changed. It's simply that each of the ideas expressed by those modifiers has either a dependent or independent clause all to itself.

> ~~Highly intelligent~~ Morris **is a highly intelligent cat**, but **when the video tapings get lengthy,** he can occasionally forget his lines. ~~during lengthy video tapings.~~

Or:

> ~~Highly intelligent~~ **Although he is** highly intelligent, Morris can occasionally forget his lines when the tapings become lengthy.

> The ~~brief~~ meeting was **brief** but highly productive.

Or:

Although the ~~brief~~ meeting was **brief, it was** highly productive.

The ~~noisy~~ restaurant **is noisy, but it** ~~graciously~~ serves great food, and does so graciously.

A FINAL LOOK

The final example in this chapter illustrates how each of the emphasis-related techniques I have been describing for you can be put to productive use in a paragraph that cries out for shading.

Spend some time with this example. Compare how the same pieces of information have been expressed in each version. Pay particularly close attention to how many of the bits of information that were expressed as modifiers in the original version are expressed as independent clauses in the edited version. And notice, finally, that none of the *lengthy* clauses in that version are dependent.

ORIGINAL
While the difficult problem of controlling emotional responses during the regularly scheduled food fights is something that most employees in our company face, the misguided, over-lengthy, and poorly administered food-fight training program, which doesn't relate to the environment in our company, isn't working. Some of the role-playing exercises are fun.

EDITED
~~While the difficult problem of controlling emotional responses during weekly food fights is something~~

~~that~~ Most employees in our company **are having trouble controlling their emotional responses during the weekly food fights,** ~~face,~~ **but the newly launched** ~~misguided, poorly administered, and over-lengthy~~ food-fight training program ~~which has just been launched doesn't relate to our company's environment~~ **isn't working. Although some of the role-playing exercises are fun, the program doesn't relate to our environment. It is also poorly administered and too long.** ~~Some of the role playing exercises are fun.~~

14

Keep Your Readers in the Loop

You would assume, wouldn't you, that once you had checked to see that all the information in a paragraph fed into the same umbrella thought, and you had then gone to the trouble of launching the paragraph with an umbrella sentence, you would no longer need to lose any sleep over a reader's ability or inability to follow the train of your thought throughout the paragraph.

Think again. For even with a unifying umbrella thought and an umbrella sentence that spells out the thought in Las Vegas neon, there's still a worrisome chance that your readers—including *summa cum laude* graduates of Evelyn Wood Reading Dynamics—will lose their way. The reason? They may lose the connection as they move from one sentence to the next.

The following paragraph, taken from a business journal published for entrepreneurs, illustrates the kind of connection-related problem I'm talking about. The paragraph is about distribution agreements, and the umbrella thought, as spelled out in the opening sentence, is that when you are negotiating these agreements, it is not usually in your best interests to insist upon exclusivity. Whether this advice is valid or not, I don't know. But I can tell you without hesitation that the wording and structure of this paragraph is not in the best interests of the people reading it.

You should think twice before you insist on exclusivity in the distribution agreements you set up with product owners. Arrangements that are non-exclusive do not take nearly as much time to negotiate. Regardless of the medium, in some fields, such as popular music or film, it is almost unheard of to gain unlimited distribution rights. When it is absolutely essential to your market strategy is the only time you should insist on it in a distribution agreement.

Unless you specialize in copyright law, it is unlikely that you found this paragraph smooth sailing. The message eventually comes through, but you have to bear down to follow the writer's train of thought. And no wonder, in light of how the sentences are worded. The problems begin at the start of the *second* sentence:

You should think twice before you insist on exclusivity in the distribution agreements you set up with product owners. Arrangements that are non-exclusive...

I see what the writer wanted to do in this second sentence. By emphasizing how much more time it takes to negotiate distribution agreements that call for exclusivity, he wanted to draw a contrast between exclusive and non-exclusive distribution agreements, But his decision to begin the second sentence with an idea we hadn't yet been introduced to—"arrangements that are non-exclusive"—presupposes that we would know ahead of time what he intended to do.

My question is, how could we have known this? When I went through this paragraph for the first time, for instance, I was temporarily disoriented. It wasn't until I reached the end of the sentence that I was able to get back on track.

Look now at the third sentence—and, in particular, at the number of words you have to work your way through before you get to a phrase—"unlimited distribution rights"— that relates directly to the umbrella thought of the paragraph. True, you are able to tie things together once you've reached the end of the sentence, but it's a struggle. Who needs it?

HOW TO KEEP READERS CONNECTED

The readability problems that plague the paragraph we've just looked at illustrate what can happen when you fail to appreciate how perilously easy it is for readers to lose their way. With this hazard in mind, look at the edited version of the same paragraph, and notice in particular the wording at the start of each sentence. It represents a technique I call "looping back."

> You should think twice before you insist on exclusivity in the distribution agreements you set up with product owners. Distribution agreements that call for exclusivity take much more time to negotiate than non-exclusive agreements. And exclusivity in some fields, such as popular music or film, is almost unheard of. The only time you should insist upon exclusivity in a distribution agreement is when it is absolutely essential to your market strategy.

If you analyze this paragraph, you will notice that at the start of the second, third, and final sentences, you run into a word or phrase that "loops back"—that is, refers directly to an idea discussed in the previous sentence. Notice, too, that in the second sentence of the edited version, the idea that exclusive distribution agreements take longer to negotiate than non-exclusive agreements still gets communicated, but that clause that refers to non-exclusive agreements— "arrangements that are non-exclusive"—no longer sits at the beginning of the sentence. It's been moved to end of the sentence, replaced by a phrase that connects directly to the idea introduced in the first sentence. Here's a closer look:

> You should think twice before you insist on exclusivity in the distribution agreements you set up with product owners. ~~Arrangements that are non-exclusive.~~ **Distribution agreements** [loops back to "distribution agreements"] **that call for exclusivity** ~~do not take nearly as much time to negotiate.~~ **take much more time to negotiate than non-exclusive agreements.** ~~Regardless of the medium, exclusivity~~ **And exclusivity** [loops back to "exclusivity"] **in some fields, such as popular music or film,** is almost unheard of. ~~When it is absolutely essential to your market strategy is the only time you should seek this feature in a distribution agreement.~~ **The only time you should insist upon exclusivity in a distribution agreement is** when it is absolutely essential to your market strategy.

The surgery performed on this paragraph represents a fairly heavy-handed use of looping back. And I am not advocating that you begin every sentence with a word or phrase that either repeats or explicitly refers to an idea in the previous sentence. More often than not, in fact, your readers will be able to make the sentence-to-sentence connection without this sort of help.

Consider the following example:

> The lunch I had yesterday at Geraldo's Hideaway was wonderful. The onion soup was so good that I bribed the waiter in order to get the recipe.

Even without a direct mention in the second sentence of "lunch," we have no trouble connecting the onion soup recipe to the lunch at Geraldo's Hideaway. Be careful, though. What may seem to *you* to be an obvious connection may not be obvious to your readers, as exemplified by this slightly altered version of the last example:

> The lunch I had yesterday at Geraldo's Hideaway was wonderful. The recipe was something I begged the owner for after I ate the onion soup.

The connection between the ideas expressed in these two sentences is not nearly as implicit as it was in the earlier example. "Recipe" doesn't connect directly to "restaurant." It's needs "onion soup" to make the connection. That's why, when you came across the words "the recipe," a voice in your brain probably piped, "Recipe? For *what*?"

This is precisely the kind of inner dialogue you *don't* want to stir up in the minds of your readers. So, when in doubt, play it safe: Make the connection as directly and as explicitly as you can.

PUTTING THE TECHNIQUE TO USE

You can loop back to an idea in the previous sentence in three different ways:

➤ Repeat a key word in the previous sentence
➤ Use a synonym to summarize the idea
➤ Use a pronoun

None of these options is inherently superior to the other, and you should be able to use all three. Here's what you need to know about each option.

Repeating a key word in the previous sentence.

Repeating a key word in the previous sentence is the simplest and most direct way to keep your readers in the loop. I know. You were told way back when that repeating words is the surest way to end up in editorial purgatory. But as I mentioned in Chapter 7, going out of your way *not* to repeat words can be counter-productive for both you and your readers. You need to distinguish between repetition that is truly repetitive (using the same modifier or expression over and over and over and over, for example) from repetition that is both logical and necessary, given your reader's need to stay connected to the flow of ideas in a paragraph.

The following examples should illustrate how the *absence* of repetition can disrupt the flow of ideas, and how deliberate use of repetition solves the problem:

ORIGINAL
Duplico Inc. unconditionally guarantees every copier it sells. Technicians repair the machine for free if it isn't working right.

EDITED
Duplico Inc. unconditionally guarantees every copier it sells. ~~Technicians repair the machine for no charge~~ If ~~it~~ **the copier** isn't working right, our technicians repair it for free.

ORIGINAL
In 1870, Harlon McGee was introduced to a Montana cattle rancher named Wade Russell, who was building a huge ant farm near Missoula. Recognizing that he couldn't handle the job on his own, he signed on as Russell's foreman.

EDITED

In 1870, Harlon McGee was introduced to a Montana cattle rancher named Wade Russell, who was building a huge ant farm near Missoula. **McGee recognized** ~~Recognizing~~ that ~~he~~ **Russell** couldn't handle the job on his own, so he signed on as Russell's foreman.

Summarizing with a synonym

If the focal point of the previous sentence is an *idea*, rather than a *word*, try to launch the second sentence with a word or phrase that sums up that idea. Examples:

ORIGINAL

Wallpaper stores across the United States are being invaded by a crazed breed of do-it-yourselfers determined to transform their homes into designer showcases. Magazines are publishing an increasing number of articles that make wallpaper hanging seem simple.

EDITED

Wallpaper stores across the United States are being invaded by a crazed breed of do-it-yourselfers determined to transform their lackluster homes into designer showcases. **The trend is being fueled by the fact that** magazines are publishing an increasing number of articles that make wallpaper hanging seem simple.

ORIGINAL

Corliss and Evans worked together for nearly 25 years before Evans decided he wanted to open up a used ukulele shop in Nova Scotia. There was a great deal of astonishment on the part of everyone.

EDITED

Corliss and Evans worked together for nearly 25 years before Evans decided he wanted open up a used ukulele shop in Nova Scotia. **The break-up of their partnership astonished everyone.** ~~There was a great deal of astonishment on the part of everyone.~~

Looping back with pronouns

Pronouns work quite well as looping back devices, just as long as the pronoun/referent connection is clear.

ORIGINAL

Tens of thousands of companies throughout the world are in the recruiting business. Helping organizations attract and screen candidates plays an important role in the hiring process of companies of every size and in virtually every industry.

EDITED

Tens of thousands of companies throughout the world are in the recruiting business. **They help** ~~Helping~~ organizations attract and screen candidates. **They also play** ~~plays~~ an important role in the hiring process of companies of every size and in virtually every industry.

But not:

> Tens of thousands of companies throughout the world offer recruiting services. **They** [the "companies" or the "services"?] help organizations attract and screen candidates.

A FINAL LOOK

The last two examples in this chapter will give you two additional glimpses of looping back in action. The first set of examples involves a paragraph from a *New York Times Sunday Magazine* article about memory, by Stephen S. Hall. The original version of that paragraph is followed by a doctored version in which I've purposely "unhooked" all of Hall's connections.

The second set of examples begins with a student paragraph that is "unhooked" throughout, followed by an edited version that establishes the connections with each of the looping back devices we've been looking at in this chapter.

> STEPHEN S. HALL
> Three years ago, two biologists at Cold Spring Harbor Laboratory on Long Island, Tim Tully and Jerry Yin, created a fruit fly that exhibits the equivalent of a photographic memory. They achieved this feat by prodding the activity of a single gene called CREB, which functions as a kind of master switch that unlocks dozens of other genes. Those liberated genes seem to do the heavy lifting in nerve cells to convert recent experience into long-term memory.

DOCTORED (WITHOUT LOOPING BACK)
Three years ago, two biologists at Cold Spring Harbor Laboratory on Long Island, Tim Tully and Jerry Yin, created a fruit fly that exhibits the equivalent of a photographic memory. Prodding the activity of a single gene called CREB, which functions as a kind of master switch that unlocks dozens of other genes, was their accomplishment. They do the heavy lifting in nerve cells to convert recent experience into long-term memory.

A CLOSER LOOK
Three years ago, two biologists at Cold Spring Harbor Laboratory on Long Island, Tim Tully and Jerry Yin, created a fruit fly that exhibits the equivalent of a photographic memory. **They achieved this feat by** prodding the activity of a single gene called CREB, which functions as a kind of master switch that unlocks dozens of other genes.~~was their main accomplishment. They~~ **Those liberated genes** seem to do the heavy lifting in nerve cells to convert recent experience into long-term memory.

ORIGINAL (WITHOUT LOOPING BACK)
Our local government has a parking policy that inconveniences residents during snow storms. The snow plow needs to clear two lanes. You are obliged to park on only one side of the street, which is a problem. People on the other side of the street can't get their cars out because of the huge blocks of ice and snow.

EDITED

Our local government has a parking policy that inconveniences residents during snow storms. The policy obliges residents to park on only one side of the street so that the snow plow can clear two lanes. The problem with this policy, though, is that the snow plow creates huge blocks of ice and snow, and people on the other side of the street can't get their cars out.

A CLOSER LOOK

Our local government has a parking policy that inconveniences residents during snow storms. **The policy obliges residents** to park on only one side of the street **so that the** snow plow ~~needs to~~ **can** clear two lanes. ~~You are obliged to park on only one side of the street, which is a problem.~~ The problem with **this policy, though, is that the snow plow creates huge blocks of ice and snow, and** people on the other side of the street can't get their cars out.

15

Use Signposts to Smooth Out the Reader's Ride

C hief among the skills that differentiate people whose writing flows smoothly from people whose writing seems to chug along in fits and starts is the ability to put to strategic use words and phrases that are commonly referred to as "transitional," but that I have long referred to as "signposts." Whatever you choose to call them, however, these devices are among the most useful tools in your editing tool kit. If you cannot integrate signposts into your paragraphs, it will be pretty much impossible for you to express your ideas in simply constructed sentences without wreaking havoc on the pace and the rhythm of that paragraph.

As the term implies, signposts tell readers where the ideas in a paragraph are *heading*. A signpost, for example (speaking of signposts), can signal to the reader that the next several words are about to express an idea that exemplifies an idea that has been introduced in the preceding sentence. Or, it can alert your reader to the fact that an idea or image is about to be amended, clarified, or contradicted.

Barry Tarshis

Do readers really need this help? Not always, and certainly not when the relationship between ideas is implicit in the wording, as in the following paragraph:

> Archie did his best to patch things up with Betty. He wrote letters. He left messages on his voice mail. He sent flowers. Nothing worked.

This paragraph doesn't need any signposts to help readers follow the ebb and flow of ideas. The relationships between the ideas expressed in each sentence are clear. Signposts would have added only clutter, as in:

> Archie did his best to patch things up with Betty. He wrote letters, **for example**. He **also** left messages on his voice mail. **In addition**, he sent flowers. **Still and all**, nothing worked.

This is signpost overkill—a syndrome found in the works of many eighteenth-century British essayists and sometimes in the works of twentieth-century writers determined to emulate the discursive, highly parenthetical style of eighteenth-century British essayists.

But there's a signpost-related condition that is just as bad. You might call it signpost "underkill," and its prevalence in certain business organizations stems from a handful of business writing instructional programs that go out of their way to *discourage* business people from using signposts. "Too many zero words" is the way one executive put it when he handed me back the manuscript of a procedures manual that I'd written for his company. Because I had been instructed to write the manual in a user-friendly and conversational tone, I'd gone out of my way to *include* signposts. He went out his way to get rid of just about all of them.

Goofy thinking, to my mind. Yes, purging signposts can shave a word of two from your sentences. Carried to extremes, though, banning signposts from your writing will lobotomize the rhythm of your sentences and, just as bad, create an abrupt, impersonal tone. Here's an example of a paragraph that fits this description:

> Difficulties in the new employee hot-tub initiative are increasing. The budget is out of control. The etiquette handbook is two weeks behind schedule. Employee tempers are flaring. The health inspector is becoming impatient. The company president wants the initiative to move forward.

You don't find *any* "zero" words in this paragraph—nothing to tell you how the ideas in the paragraph relate to one another. But neither do you find a paragraph that flows very smoothly. And the information conveyed in the last sentence of the paragraph comes out of the blue. Look what happens, though, when you deftly integrate this paragraph with a handful of signposts.

> Difficulties in the new employee hot-tub initiative are increasing. The budget, **for example**, is out of control, and the etiquette handbook is two weeks behind schedule. **Worse,** employee tempers are flaring, **and** the health inspector is getting impatient. **Still and all**, the company president is insisting that the initiative move forward.

Here's another before-and-after example of how the deft use of signposts can influence the rhythm of a paragraph. The first of the two paragraphs below comes from a Frank Deford profile of Larry Bird. The second is a doctored version in which all of Deford's "zero" words have been sacrificed, along with all the nuance found in the original version.

ORIGINAL

Evidently what we see of him in public, working at his vocation, is an extension of the person. It hasn't always been easy to understand this, though, because Bird is an exceptionally private man. Of course, every celebrity loves to swear that he's really very shy. It's an appealing lie. But Bird is shy.

DOCTORED

Evidently what we see of him in public, working at his vocation, is an extension of the person. It hasn't always been easy to understand this. ~~though, because~~ Bird is an exceptionally private man. ~~Of course,~~ Every celebrity loves to swear that he's really very shy. It's an appealing lie. ~~But~~ Bird is shy.

You may have noticed in the original version of the preceding two paragraphs, Deford did something that students in writing classes have long been told *never* to do, which is to begin a sentence with *but* (not to mention *and*.) But as William Zinsser advises in *On Writing Well*, "If that's what you learned, unlearn it. There is no stronger word at the start."

Granted, you don't want to start *too many* of your sentences with either of these words, but as you will see from the examples you'll be reading throughout this chapter, *and* and *but* are two of the most versatile signposts you can use, *especially* at the beginning of a sentence.

PUTTING SIGNPOSTS TO WORK

To use signposts effectively, you need to be able to do two things: First of all, you need to be able to recognize when they're needed—or, more precisely, when their absence is taking a toll on either the logic or the flow of the writing. You must then be able to decide which particular signpost ought to be pressed into action.

The first of these skills is impossible to teach: It's all about "ear," or "feel"—an attribute akin to what stand-up comics call "timing." Some writers and editors (perhaps because they enjoy *reading*) can sense instinctively when the writing is too choppy. They *hear* it. Other writers recognize the need for signposts only when the choppiness reaches tidal wave proportions.

But once you've isolated a sequence of sentences that could use a signpost or two, the challenge eases considerably. That's because signposts can be divided into several discrete categories, based on the relationships they're meant to signal.

Here's a look at four of the most common of these categories, followed first by a list of signposts that fall into each category and then with before-and-after examples that show these signposts at work.

PROVING YOUR POINT

The following signposts are among the many that tell your readers that you're about to *illustrate* a point that has just been introduced:

for example	by way of illustration
to begin with	let's say
to illustrate	say
for instance	for one thing

ORIGINAL
The screenwriter has taken several liberties with the original material. Hamlet now works as a volleyball instructor at a nudist camp.

EDITED

The screenwriter has taken several liberties with the original material. Hamlet, **for example**, now works as a volleyball instructor at a nudist camp.

ORIGINAL

You can structure this particular insurance plan in any number of different ways. If you want the coverage to extend to your polo ponies, but not your reptile collection, you may do so.

EDITED

You can structure this particular insurance plan in any number of different ways. If, **let's say**, you want the coverage to extend to your polo ponies, but not your reptile collection, you may do so.

ORIGINAL

Tensions started to build between Vera and Mike as soon as they brought the python home. They discovered that the python liked to sleep on their bed when they weren't home.

EDITED

Tensions started to build between Vera and Mike as soon as they brought the python home. **For one thing**, they discovered that the python liked to sleep on their bed when they weren't home.

ADDING HEAT

The following signposts tell your readers that you're about to amend or reinforce an idea that has just been expressed:

and	also
in fact	indeed by
the same token	worse
what's more	beyond this
in addition	in fact
moreover	better still
then, too	yet another
not only that, but	even worse

ORIGINAL
The screenwriter has taken several liberties with the original material. He has rewritten the entire play.

EDITED
The screenwriter has taken several liberties with the original material. **Indeed,** he has rewritten the entire play.

Or:

The screenwriter has taken several liberties with the original material. He has, **in fact**, rewritten the entire play.

ORIGINAL
You can structure this particular insurance plan in any number of ways. You can choose from many options that weren't available last year.

EDITED
You can structure this insurance plan in any number of ways. **What's more,** you can choose from many options that weren't available last year.

ORIGINAL

Tensions started to build between Vera and Mike as soon as they brought the python home. They weren't able to talk openly about these tensions when the snake was in the room.

EDITED

Tensions started to build between Vera and Mike as soon as they brought the python home. **Worse,** they weren't able to talk openly about these tensions when the snake was in the room.

CHANGING DIRECTIONS

The following signposts tell your readers that you're about to qualify or contradict an idea that you've just introduced:

all the same	nevertheless
by way of contrast	no matter
either	nonetheless
on the other hand	even though
still	granted
then again	however
even so	in spite of
true	instead
yet	by contrast

ORIGINAL

The screenwriter has done some nice things with the original material. The script lacks originality.

EDITED

The screenwriter has done some nice things with the original material. **Even so**, the script lacks originality.

ORIGINAL

You can structure this insurance plan in any number of ways. It's a simple plan to use.

EDITED

You can structure this insurance plan in any number of ways. **Nonetheless,** it's a simple plan to use.

ORIGINAL

Tensions started to build between Vera and Mike as soon as they brought the python home. None of their friends had any inkling that anything was wrong.

EDITED

Tensions started to build between Vera and Mike as soon as they brought the python home. **Yet,** none of their friends had any inkling that anything was wrong.

Or:

Tensions started to build between Vera and Mike as soon as they brought the python home. None of their friends, **however,** had any inkling that anything was wrong.

CITING CONSEQUENCES

The following signposts tell your readers you're about to report the consequences of an idea you've just presented:

accordingly	as a result
because of this	consequently
hence	so
thus	therefore
ergo	because of this

ORIGINAL
The screenwriter has taken several liberties with the original material. You don't recognize most of Shakespeare's characters.

EDITED
The screenwriter has taken several liberties with the original material. **Consequently**, you don't recognize most of Shakespeare's characters.

ORIGINAL
You can participate in this insurance plan in any number of ways.You can't go wrong.

EDITED
You can participate in this insurance plan in any number of ways. **As a result**, you can't go wrong.

ORIGINAL
Tensions started to build between Vera and Mike as soon as they brought the python home. It was no surprise that Vera began to grind her teeth.

Edited

Tensions started to build between Vera and Mike as soon as they brought the python home. **So** it was no surprise that Vera began to grind her teeth.

GETTING THE MOST OUT OF SIGNPOSTS

Apart from being able to recognize when a signpost is called for, and which category should be the source of it, two other points about signposts are worth stressing before we move on.

Point number one (to repeat the point I mentioned earlier) is to use them in moderation. Keep in mind that if you overuse signposts, they will *impede*, not enhance, the flow of the writing.

Point number two is to pay attention to where you place them in the paragraph. Signposts don't necessarily have to come at the *beginning* of a sentence. Frequently, in fact (as in *this* sentence), the sentence will flow more smoothly if you insert the signpost after either the first word or the first few words, as the following examples illustrate:

Original

Jennings uncovered several financial irregularities during his visit. **For example**, he discovered that the bank president had built a hot tub in the vault.

Edited

Jennings uncovered several financial irregularities during his visit. ~~For example,~~ He discovered, **for example**, that the bank president had built a hot tub in the vault.

ORIGINAL

Thanksgiving at the Brady house this year was unusually rowdy. **In fact**, it was the rowdiest Thanksgiving since Marcia got out of prison.

EDITED

Thanksgiving at the Brady house this year was unusually rowdy. ~~In fact,~~ It was, **in fact,** the rowdiest Thanksgiving since Marcia got out of prison.

ORIGINAL

Evan did his best over the next few weeks to keep his business going. **However,** he gradually began to realize that there is no market in America for guacamole raisin crunch ice cream.

EDITED

Evan did his best over the next few weeks to keep his business going. ~~However, he~~ Gradually, **however,** he began to realize that there is no market in America for guacamole raisin crunch ice cream.

GETTING INTO THE SIGNPOST GROOVE

The best way to get good at incorporating signposts into your writing is to analyze how accomplished writers use them, and to learn from their example. A good source of paragraphs liberally seeded with signposts are the weekly news magazines, like *Time, Newsweek,* and *U.S. News and World Report*. But you can pick up just about any carefully edited magazine or newspaper, and you will find good examples to learn from.

When you find such a paragraph, read it not just once but again and again, paying attention to not only *which* sign-posts are used but where in the paragraph or sentence they have been inserted.

The following sets of paragraphs should get you started in this learning process. Each set gives you two versions of the same paragraph: one without signposts, and the other with signposts.

ORIGINAL

Studies show that business could save as much as 75 percent of their lighting bills with systems that automatically turn off lights when people leave such areas as private offices, hallways, and toilets. The electronic systems assigned to detect human comings and goings sometimes turn off lights even when people haven't left an area. Business has been slow to adopt this quirky technology.

EDITED

Studies show that business could save as much as 75 percent of their lighting bills with systems that automatically turn off lights when people leave such areas as private offices, hallways, and toilets. **But** the electronic systems assigned to detect human comings and goings sometimes turn off lights even when people haven't left an area. **As a result,** business has been slow to adopt this quirky technology.

ORIGINAL

Jason Smith's work reaffirms the suspicion that work performance differences between night shift and day shift workers are rooted in the light-related misalignment of the circadian rhythm and the sleep problems that result from this misalignment.

His work indicates that, to some extent at least, these problems can be minimized. Smith has been careful to emphasize that many important questions remain unanswered. He has yet to determine which is more significant to circadian adaptation: bright light during night work or darkness during daylight sleep.

EDITED

Jason Smith's work reaffirms the suspicion that work performance differences between night shift and day shift workers are rooted in the light-related misalignment of the circadian rhythm and the sleep problems that result from this misalignment. His work **also** indicates that, to some extent at least, these problems can be minimized, **but** he has been careful to emphasize that a number of important questions remain unanswered. He has yet to determine, **for instance**, which is more significant to circadian adaptation: bright light during night work or darkness during daylight sleep.

ORIGINAL

The workshop will focus on goofing-off tactics for lazy employees. It will emphasize a strategic approach to not getting caught. It will review the factors that under-lie successful malingering. It will enable participants to develop cool responses to questions from supervisors who put on the heat.

EDITED

The workshop will focus on goofing-off tactics for lazy employees. It will emphasize, **for instance**, a strategic approach to not getting caught, and will review the factors that underlie successful malingering. It will **also** enable participants to develop cool responses to questions likely to come up when supervisors begin to put on the pressure.

16

Create Mini-umbrellas for Complex Information

I t is a basic principle of nutrition that certain foods, by virtue of their composition, texture, and density, take longer to chew and digest than others. The same principle applies to writing. Sort of.

Here's my point: How easy or difficult it is for readers to work their way through your sentences is not so much a function of how many *words* they have to process. Rather, it is the number and the complexity of the thoughts that those words are meant to communicate, and, equally important, how familiar your readers are with the topics and the ideas you're writing about. The more complex and unfamiliar the information, the more time your readers need to absorb each individual morsel of information—and the more important it becomes for you to deliver that information in carefully controlled portions.

Which brings me to an advanced but highly versatile editing technique that I call the "umbrella phrase."

SETTING THE STAGE

Like the umbrella sentence, which we covered in Chapter 5, an umbrella phrase sets the stage for information that lies ahead.

The only difference is that umbrella phrases are more limited in their scope. Instead of setting the stage for an entire paragraph, an umbrella phrase sets the stage for information communicated in only one or, at most, three or four sentences. As such, you can use several umbrella phrases throughout a paragraph, as the need arises, as long as you show some restraint.

The following set of paragraphs will illustrate for you the value of this tool. The first example is a long and sprawling sentence that desperately needs to be broken into smaller chunks. The second example illustrates how that sentence would read if you did nothing else but express the ideas in individual sentences. The final version is an edited version in which I have inserted two umbrella phrases.

ORIGINAL
The minimal effect that dieting has on the capacity of so-called "fat" cells to produce obesity is the result of its reduction effect on the size of the cells rather than the number of cells, in addition to which the depletion of fat caused by dieting, some researchers now believe, actually triggers the urge to eat until the fat is restored.

EDITED (WITHOUT UMBRELLA PHRASES)
~~The minimal effect that~~ Dieting has **a minimal effect** on the capacity of so-called "fat" cells to produce obesity. ~~is the result of its reduction effect on the~~ Dieting doesn't reduce ~~size of the cells rather than~~ the number of cells. **It simply reduces their size.**

~~in addition to which the depletion of fat~~ Dieting **appears to deplete the state of fat in these cells.** ~~caused by dieting~~ **And** some researchers now believe **that this depletion** actually triggers the urge to eat until the fat is restored.

145

EDITED (WITH UMBRELLA PHRASES)
Dieting has a minimal effect on the capacity of so-called "fat" cells to produce obesity—**and for two reasons: First**, dieting doesn't reduce the number of these cells in the body; it simply reduces their size. **Second**, dieting appears to deplete the state of fat in these cells. And some researchers now believe that this depletion **does the last thing a person trying to lose weight needs: It** actually triggers the urge to eat until the fat is restored.

You may have noticed that the two umbrella phrases in the preceding example perform slightly different functions. The first of the two phrases—"and for two r easons"— enhances clarity by letting the reader know that the two pieces of information that lie ahead are "reasons" why dieting has a minimal effect on the so-called "fat" cells.

The second of the umbrella phrases—"does the last thing a person trying to lose weight needs"— does something else: It creates suspense. It grabs the reader's attention. It plants in the reader's mind the following question: "What is the last thing a person trying to lose weight needs?"

PUTTING UMBRELLA PHRASES TO WORK

Whether you use umbrella phrases to enhance clarity or to build suspense, the key to using them effectively is being able to pick your spots—recognizing when it makes sense to insert these phrases, and when their presence would simply slow down the writing. Here's a closer look at how to use the technique in each of these situations:

Setting up a series

A good rule of thumb is to use an umbrella phrase whenever you're about to deliver three or more chunks of related information in a series. Some examples:

ORIGINAL
The newly elected representative came to Washington determined to balance the budget, lower taxes, reduce the size of government, and find a loving home for his pet hamster.

EDITED
The newly elected representative came to Washington **determined to accomplish four things:** balance the budget, lower taxes, reduce the size of government, and find a loving home for his pet hamster.

ORIGINAL
In its efforts to improve employee morale, the company has relaxed the dress code, increased the number of personal days from five to eight, and started construction on a rooftop employee hot tub.

EDITED
In its efforts to improve employee morale, the company **has taken three steps:** it has relaxed the dress code, increased the number of personal days from five to eight, and started construction on a rooftop employee hot tub.

ORIGINAL

We would feel a lot happier about these negotiations if it weren't for the cramped meeting room, the long hours, and the money we're paying our lawyers.

EDITED

We would feel a lot happier about these negotiations if it weren't for **three factors:** the cramped meeting room, the long hours, and the money we're paying our lawyers.

Creating suspense

If you want an umbrella phrase to not only announce the imminent arrival of information but also to create suspense, you have to do more than simply insert a phrase. You usually have to rearrange sentence elements and, in some cases, come up with a word or two that creates a provocative question in the reader's mind. Consider the following examples:

ORIGINAL

As companies expand their base of personal computers and local area networks, it is becoming apparent that the complexity of these environments is much greater than anticipated.

EDITED

As companies expand their base of personal computers and local area networks, **one thing is becoming apparent:** the complexity of these environments is much greater than anticipated.

Or:

ORIGINAL
The only hitch in the arrangements we've made is that nobody knows what time the tango lessons start.

EDITED
The arrangements we've made **have only one hitch**: Nobody knows what time the tango lessons start.

There's **only one hitch to these arrangements:** Nobody knows what time the tango lessons start.

ORIGINAL
Essential as it is for the body to supply the brain and spinal cord with blood, the process is nonetheless limited in that there is a need to protect the brain from foreign substances.

EDITED
Essential as it is for body to supply the brain and spinal cord with blood **the process is limited by one critical priority:** the need to protect the brain from foreign substances.

A FINAL LOOK

The last two examples in this chapter do a nice job of illustrating how umbrella phrases can make complicated subjects seem more accessible. The first set of examples comes from the first draft of a psychology textbook I co-wrote many years ago. The second comes from a book on rhetoric. The content in both paragraphs is complicated, but that's why I've chosen them as examples.

ORIGINAL

The entry of calcium into the neuron marks the beginning of the process that underlies the actual structural change that takes place inside the neuron, in which after entering the neuron, calcium initiates a chemical reaction that activates an enzyme and produces a change in protein structure.

EDITED

The entry of calcium into the neuron ~~marks the beginning of~~ **launches** the process that underlies the actual structural change in the neuron. ~~in which.~~ **The process goes roughly as follows:** After entering the neuron, calcium initiates a chemical reaction that **consists of two steps: first, it** ~~that~~ activates an enzyme; ~~and~~ **second,** ~~and~~ it ~~produces a change in~~ **changes** the protein structure.

ORIGINAL

A third category of rules concerns the form that concepts and theories must assume to be accepted as knowledge in the discourse. Some rules, for example, govern the arrangements of statements necessary in order for the discourse to be seen as making a contribution to knowledge, while others dictate a style and form of that discourse. Other rules determine which terms will be recognized as valid, which will be questionable, and which will be invalid. They specify the kind of discourse in which the highest truth resides by indicating which statements are true and which are false.

EDITED

A third category of rules **introduces yet another concern**—concerns the form that concepts and theories must assume to be accepted as knowledge in the discourse. Some rules, for example, govern the arrangements of statements necessary in order for the discourse to be seen as making a contribution to knowledge, while others dictate a style and form of that discourse. Other rules determine **three things:** which terms will be recognized as valid, which will be questionable, and which will be invalid. **And these rules do something else as well: by indicating which statements are true and which are false,** they specify the kind of discourse in which the highest truth resides. ~~by indicating which statements are true and which are false.~~

17

Put Parallelism into Practice

Parallelism—also known as parallel structure—is the technical term for any arrangement of sentence parts in which words and phrases that do the same *job* (i.e., express an action, modify the same word, etc.) are also expressed in the same grammatical uniform, as in Hamlet's famous question— "To be or not to be?"—or Caesar's famous declaration—"I came, I saw, I conquered."

Parallelism has no measurable impact on brevity or conciseness, but it sure does bear strongly how *smoothly* the writing flows, as the following examples amply demonstrate:

NOT PARALLEL
A government of the people, that people have organized, and that is responsive to people.

PARALLEL
A government of the people, by the people, and for the people.

NOT PARALLEL
Neither a lender be, and don't borrow, either.

PARALLEL

Neither a lender nor borrower be.

NOT PARALLEL

...we shall fight on the landing grounds, we intend to engage the enemy in the fields, and also the streets. The hills will also be a place we'll fight. Surrender is something we will never do.

PARALLEL

...we shall fight on the landing grounds, we shall fight in the fields, and in the streets, we shall fight in the hills; we shall never surrender.

Your ear should tell you that something is amiss in the "not parallel" versions of each of these sentences. But if your ear doesn't sound the alarm, you can also rely on your eyes— assuming, that is, you're up to speed on the parts of speech (not to mention the different types of phrases that arise from each part of speech).

In the "parallel" version of the first of the preceding examples, for instance, the three groups of words that follow "A government" are all prepositional phrases, each ending with "people." In the "not parallel" version, only one of the word groupings is a prepositional phrase—"of the people." The other two ideas are expressed in clauses, each with a different subject and verb. Similar consistencies and inconsistencies are also found in the other two examples.

Without getting mired in the technicalities of syntax, it should be pointed out that different combinations of grammatical structures in the same series can produce different degrees of bumpiness and awkwardness, depending on the mix of structures. Which is simply another way of saying that a sentence lacking in parallel structure doesn't *always* need to be retooled: The litmus test is how awkwardly and bumpily the sentence *reads*, its structure notwithstanding.

It's also worth noting that parallelism works better in certain forms of writing than in others. It is particularly well suited to prose that is meant to be *spoken* (or sung), as evidenced by the parallel structure that dominates poetry, and evidenced, too, by the parallel structure that characterizes the most memorable passages from great speeches throughout history. Be on guard, though: Too much parallelism in your writing can make your writing too contrived and too mannered.

A CLOSER LOOK

The examples that follow are meant to give you a general idea of how the *lack* of parallelism in sentences can break up the flow of a sentence. Each example consists of three components: (1) a sentence that *lacks* parallel structure; (2) a grammatical analysis of that sentence; and (3) an edited version in which the non-parallel elements of the sentence have been expressed in the same grammatical form.

ORIGINAL
Herman Hancock has always preached that the best way to succeed in the left-handed tool business is to work hard, that you should focus on the fundamentals, and enjoying yourself.

ANALYSIS
Herman Hancock has always preached that the best way to succeed in the left-handed tool business is **to work hard** [infinitive phrase], **that you should focus on the fundamentals** [dependent clause], and **enjoying yourself** [gerund].

PARALLEL

Herman Hancock has always preached that the best way to succeed in the left-handed tool business is **to work hard,** ~~that you should~~ **to focus on the fundamentals, and** ~~enjoying~~ **to enjoy yourself** [three infinitive phrases].

Or:

Herman Hancock has always preached that the best way to succeed in the left-handed tool business is ~~to work~~ **by working hard,** ~~that you should focus~~ **by focusing** on the fundamentals, and **by enjoying** yourself [three gerunds].

Or:

Herman Hancock has always preached that the best way to succeed in the left-handed tool business is ~~work hard, that you should focus on the fundamentals, and enjoying yourself.~~ **by following three principles: You work hard, you focus on the fundamentals,** and **you enjoy yourself** [three independent clauses].

ORIGINAL

The new RX5 is everything you would ever want in a stereophonic vacuum cleaner: It is fast; its responsiveness is impressive; and you will find the style attractive.

ANALYSIS

The new RX5 is everything you would ever want in a stereophonic vacuum cleaner: It's **fast** [adjective]; **its**

responsiveness is impressive [independent clause]; and **you will find the style attractive** [independent clause, with a different subject and verb].

PARALLEL
The new RX5 is everything you would ever want in a stereophonic vacuum cleaner: it's **fast,** ~~its responsiveness is impressive;~~ **responsive,** ~~and you will find the style attractive~~ and **stylish** [three adjectives operating as the complement of the sentence].

ORIGINAL
Ellen spent most of the day thinking about what she'd seen that morning at the ant farm, brooding over how she had reacted, and struggled to put her relationship with Willoughby into perspective.

ANALYSIS
Ellen spent most of the day **thinking about** [gerund] what she'd seen that morning at the ant farm, **brooding over** [gerund] how she had reacted, and **struggled** [verb] to put her relationship with Willoughby into perspective.

PARALLEL
Ellen spent most of the day **thinking about** what she'd seen that morning at the ant farm, **brooding over** how she had reacted, and ~~struggled~~ **struggling** to put her relationship with Willoughby into perspective [three gerunds].

PARALLEL STRUCTURE IN PARAGRAPHS

The basic principles of parallelism stay the same when you apply the technique to paragraphs. The only difference is that the mechanics get a little more complicated. You need to make sure, above all, that the content lends itself to parallel structure. Here are two good professionally written examples of paragraphs whose structure is pretty much parallel from start to finish.

> JOAN DIDION (FROM AN ESSAY ABOUT JOAN BAEZ)
> She lives quietly. She reads, and she talks to people who have been told where she lives, and occasionally she and Ira Sandperl go to San Francisco to see friends, to talk about the peace movement. She sees her two sisters and she sees Ira Sandperl. She believes that her days at the Institute talking and listening to Ira Sandperl are bringing her closer to contentment than anything she has done so far.

> PETER ROSS RANGE
> Japan is the most pervasively prosperous country on earth. . . . It is the country with the highest life expectancy of any nation in the world except Iceland. It is the country where trains run so perfectly on time that if you board the 12:10 for Kyoto at 12:10 and 30 seconds, you are getting onto another train using that same platform to head for someplace else. It is the country where the taxi drivers still open and shut the door for you.

You'll notice that many of the sentences in each of these paragraphs are not merely similarly structured but similarly worded as well. Look again at the Peter Ross Range paragraph. Notice that all three sentences begin with the same four words: "It is the country."

By way of contrast, look at the following paragraph, whose writer, a computer consultant, appears to have gone out of his way to use parallel structure, and with klutzy results:

> The selection of a hardware platform should be based on three factors. One key factor is that third-party boards should be interchangeable. For example, picking two platforms with differing bus architectures would force you to standardize on two separate network interface cards, sound cards, add-on disks, and CD-ROM drives. Second, choose vendors that are solid and will remain in business over the life of the product. And third, it's important that vendors' products can be maintained easily, either by your internal support staff or by local systems integrators or maintenance providers.

The problem with this paragraph is that it's totally lacking in parallelism. Each sentence has its own unique sequence of grammatical vehicles.

What do you do when you come across such a paragraph in your editing? The simplest strategy is to do what I have done in the revision that follows, which is choose one grammatical vehicle and funnel most of the information through that vehicle. You'll notice in the edited revision that most of the information comes packaged in sentences that share the same subject—you. You'll notice, too, that the same two words—"make sure"—appear throughout the paragraph.

> **When you are** choosing ~~The selection of~~ a hardware platform, three factors should dominate your thinking. ~~should be based on three factors.~~ **First,**

you should make sure ~~key factor is~~ that third-party boards are interchangeable. ~~For example, picking two platforms with differing bus architectures would force you~~ Otherwise **you're forced** to standardize on two separate network interface cards, sound cards, add-on disks, and CD-ROM drives. ~~it's important that~~ Second, **you should make sure that you** choose vendors that are solid and will remain in business over the life of the product. **Third, you need to make sure that** ~~it's important that~~ vendors' products can be maintained easily, either by your internal support staff or by local systems integrators or maintenance providers.

PARALLEL STRUCTURE: THE FINE PRINT

Parallel structure has a slightly hazardous side to it—a way of lulling an unsuspecting reader into making inappropriate connections. Here are two examples:

The scientists found that the rats gained weight on the new diet and learned that even a small increase in fat could have a major effect on weight gain.

Fly-by-Night believes that what customers want the most is today better service and trains its employees accordingly.

You see what's happening in these sentences, don't you? The parallel structure of the sentence leads you to connect the words that follow the conjunction and with the wrong subject. The rats didn't "learn" anything from the experiments; the scientists did. Fly-by-Night "trains" (a verb) people; customers don't want "trains" (a noun). More evidence yet for why it's so essential when you edit to not only *look* carefully at the writing, but also to *listen* carefully.

To correct these problems, you needn't do anything drastic. Simply add words to clarify the connection.

> The scientists found that the rats gained weight on the new diet, and **they** found as well that even a small increase in fat could have a major effect on weight gain.

> Fly-by-Night's senior management believes that what customers want the most is good service. And **the company** trains its employees accordingly.

18

Know When— and How—to Combine

C ombining is a rarity among writing and editing tools: It is *called* what it actually *does*. Combining is merging: You incorporate into a single sentence ideas and images that you conceivably could have incorporated into another sentence, or expressed as a sentence unto itself.

Some things you should know about combining:

One, it invariably *lengthens* a sentence, which means that it's not a tool you should be using with abandon if you write about complicated topics to an audience that isn't plugged into those topics.

Two, combining is a difficult tool to use when you're editing somebody else's work. The reason: The way you combine sentences is one of the defining characteristics of your particular writing style.

Three, combining is hard to do well—and even harder to teach. Here, again, you need a good ear for sentence rhythms in order to combine elements without interfering with either the clarity or the flow of the writing. Lacking this quality, your efforts to combine sentence elements could well produce sentences not unlike the one you are about to read, which appeared long ago in the arts section of one of America's most respected newspapers.

Timidly, she assured Mr. Riggio, who said she would probably like to sell more but then so would Stephen King, that she was not complaining.

This is a painful example of what happens when a writer combines sentence elements without paying enough attention to how the juxtaposition of elements will affect either rhythm *or* clarity.

What I hope to prove to you in this chapter, though, is that while it certainly helps to have a good ear for sentence rhythms, you don't need the writing equivalent of perfect pitch to learn the basics of combining. This chapter will cover the basics. The rest is up to you.

THE IMPACT OF COMBINING

To get things started, let's take a look at what combining actually *does*—that is, how it can add texture and spark to writing when it is done skillfully and in the appropriate kind of document. I've taken a paragraph from a Philip Lopate essay called "Modern Friendship," and I have presented two versions of it. The first is the paragraph as Lopate originally wrote it. The second is a doctored version in which I have "uncombined" the elements that Lopate put together so admirably in the original version.

ORIGINAL (WITH COMBINING)
Contemporary urban life, with its tight schedules and crowded appointment books, has helped to shape modern friendship into something requiring a good deal of intentionality and pursuit. You phone a friend and make a date a week or more in advance; then you set aside an evening, like a tryst, during which to squeeze in all your news and advice, confession and opinion. Such intimate compression

may add a romantic note to modern friendship, but it also places a strain on the meeting to yield a high quality of meaning and satisfaction, closer to art than life, thereby increasing the chance of disappointment. If I see certain busy or out-of-town friends only once every six months, we must not only catch up on our lives but convince ourselves within the allotted two hours together that we still share a special affinity, an inner track to each other's psyches, or the next meeting may be put off for years.

Doctored Version (Without Combining)
Contemporary urban life has tight schedules. It also has crowded appointment books. It has helped to shape modern friendship into something requiring a good deal of intentionality and pursuit. You phone a friend. You make a date a week or more in advance. You set aside an evening. It is like a tryst. During it you squeeze in all your news and advice, confession and opinion. Such intimate compression may add a romantic note to modern friendship. It also places a strain on the meeting. The meeting has to yield a high quality of meaning and satisfaction. This meaning and satisfaction is closer to art than life. It thereby increases the chance of disappointment. I see certain busy or out-of-town friends only once every six months. We must not just catch up on our lives. We must also convince ourselves within the allotted two hours together that we still share a special affinity.
This affinity is an inner track to each other's psyches. If not, the next meeting may be put off for years.

What's worth nothing about the "uncombined" version of this paragraph is that it gets off to a decent start. The first few sentences read rather nicely. It's not until you get about a third of the way into the paragraph that the relentless succession of short, identically structured sentences starts to get on your nerves, and begins to interfere with your ability to stay interested in Lopate's observations.

We need to bear in mind, of course, that this paragraph comes from a personal essay, a prose form well suited to the leisurely and lyrical rhythms that combining can produce. I would not encourage you to emulate Lopate's style in your next memo, or in any document whose purpose to purely to *inform*, such as an instructional manual written for people who earn their living defusing explosive devices.

THE NUTS AND BOLTS OF COMBINING

Complex though combining may seem on the surface, the basic dynamics are surprisingly simple.

You have only a handful of options. The trick is to know how to put those options to effective use.

Probably the simplest method of combining is to merge two separate sentences into a single sentence, leaving each sentence pretty much intact. A second—and more complicated option—is to transplant portions of one sentence somewhere within the "host" sentence as an independent clause, a dependent clause, or a modifying phrase. Here's a closer look at each option.

Creating compound sentences

A compound sentence is any sentence consisting of two (and, in rare cases, more than two) independent clauses. The clauses are usually separated by a comma and by a conjunction such as *and*, *but*, or *because*, but you can sometimes replace the comma with a semicolon. The goal, in any event, is the same: You want to keep the flow moving from one clause to the next. You don't want the kind of distinct pause that is imposed by a period. Some examples:

WITHOUT COMBINING
You can lead a horse to water. You can't make him drink.

COMPOUND SENTENCE
You can lead a horse to water, but you can't make him drink.

WITHOUT COMBINING
We all knew about the gambling going on in the kindergarten cloakroom. Nobody did anything.

COMPOUND SENTENCE
We all knew about the gambling going on in the kindergarten cloakroom, and nobody did anything.

WITHOUT COMBINING
Such intimate compression may add a romantic note to modern friendship. It also places a strain on the meeting.

COMPOUND SENTENCE
Such intimate compression may add a romantic note to modern friendship, but it also places a strain on the meeting.

Let me draw your attention to two points about the previous examples.

Point number one is that the ideas that have been combined in the compound sentences are closely related. Once combined, the two clauses form a logical tandem. Such is *not* the case in the following three examples:

> You can lead a horse to water, but the Lone Ranger's horse was named Silver.

> Everybody knew about the gambling in the kindergarten cloakroom, and the teacher had red hair.

> Such intimate compression may add a romantic note to modern friendship, and I see certain busy or out-of-town friends only once every six months.

Point number two is that even after the elements have been combined, the sentence still reads clearly. Combining doesn't interfere with the reader's ability to absorb the information, as it does in the following sentence:

> You can lead a horse, an animal that gets as thirsty as humans, to water, but you can't make, let alone induce or tempt that horse, to drink, which is a truism that can be applied to many lessons in everyday life.

Assuming, though, that clarity *won't* suffer if you merge two sentences into a compound sentence, it doesn't matter all that much whether you combine two related sentences or keep them separate. In most instances, it's a matter of personal style, and it also depends on the kind of writing you do. Essayists, as a rule, like to express their ideas in a casual, conversational tone, and tend to favor compound sentences. Newspaper reporters and business writers generally favor a sharper-edged, journalistic style, and tend to shy away from compound sentences.

The paragraphs that follow do a good job of illustrating the different "feel" produced by each option. The first example that follows comes from a paragraph in a Lewis Lapham essay, and it consists of two lengthy, but beautifully balanced and solidly constructed compound sentences. The second paragraph comes fr om Tracy Kidder's *The Soul of the Machine.* It is notable for its conspicuous *lack* of compound sentences.

LEWIS LAPHAM

The obsession with images is as evident in Los Angeles and New York as it is in Washington, but the difference in emphasis is the difference between people interested in thought and expression and people interested in power. It is the business of New York and Los Angeles to manufacture images (whimsically transforming unknown southern governors into presidential candidates), but it is the business of Washington to trade in those images as the currency of political truism.

TRACY KIDDER

The days of the debugging wore on. In March West said, referring strictly to the debugging, "Most of the worst is gone now." He was speaking only for himself, however. The team had passed through the first sharp fear. But they had designed the machine much too fast for prudence. It had features that none of the group had dealt with before. At this stage none of them dared claim to understand in detail how all the parts worked and fit together. Sufficient cause for worry about the debugging remained.

The difference between these two paragraphs has little to do with clarity. Both paragraphs are easy to read and easy to understand. The difference is rhythm and pacing. Lapham's paragraph has a fluid, leisurely pace; Kidder's paragraph has a sharper-edged, more staccato rhythm. As it happens, the information in both paragraphs lends itself to either style. Here's a look at how the information in Kidder's paragraph might have read if Lewis Lapham had edited the paragraph, followed by a look at how the information in Lapham's paragraph might have read if Kidder had written it:

KIDDER'S PARAGRAPH, LAPHAM STYLE
The days of the debugging wore on, **and** in March West said, referring strictly to the debugging, "Most of the worst is gone now." He was speaking only for himself, however. The team had passed through the first sharp fear, **but** they had designed the machine much too fast for prudence, and it had features that none of the group had dealt with before. At this stage none of them dared claim to understand in detail how all the parts worked and fit together, **and** sufficient cause for worry about the debugging remained.

LAPHAM'S PARAGRAPH, KIDDER STYLE
The obsession with images is as evident in Los Angeles and New York as it is in Washington. ~~but~~ **The** difference in emphasis is the difference between people interested in thought and expression and people interested in power. It is the business of New York and Los Angeles to manufacture images (whimsically transforming unknown southern governors into presidential candidates). ~~but~~ **It** is the business of Washington to trade in those images as the currency of political truism.

The differences between the doctored and original versions of the preceding paragraphs strike me as negligible— more a matter of style and taste than anything else. Overall, though, the lesson is this: As long as you're careful not to either overuse or underuse compound sentences, your fondness or distaste for them shouldn't undermine the fundamental readability of your writing. I rely a good deal on compound sentences in most of my writing, but I know many good writers who use them sparingly. Overall, though, my advice is to avoid extremes. Used excessively, compound sentences—particularly if they are long and complex—can make your writing unwieldy: You need to be conscious of balance and flow. Go out of your way *not* to use compound sentences, on the other hand, and your writing is likely to be too choppy.

APPOSITIVE THINKING

One of the most common and easily learned forms of combining consists of converting an idea expressed as an indeendent clause of one sentence into a dependent clause or nonessential phrase that works as an appositive (i.e., a mirror image) to the subject of the "host" sentence.

This move is fairly straightforward: The key (apart from making sure that the appositive element is, in fact, a "mirror image" of the subject) is making sure that the appositive element isn't so long and involved that it sidetracks the main idea of the sentence—an issue we'll deal with at the end of this chapter.

One final note: Appositive phrases tend to work better when they come either early in the sentence or at the end of a sentence, rather than in middle, and they can create pacing problems if you insert them in the middle of sentences. The examples that follow illustrate how the technique works. You'll note that in each of the examples below, the combined elements mesh smoothly with the original sentence—and for the two reasons I've just stressed. The appositive elements are relatively short, and they've inserted either early on the sentence or at the end.

UNCOMBINED

Vera Maxwell has been appointed president of Seascape Inc. Ms. Maxwell played Melinda, the kleptomaniac heiress, in the soap opera Edge of Our Lives.

COMBINED

Vera Maxwell, **who played the kleptomaniac heiress Melinda in the soap opera Edge of our Lives,** has been appointed president of Seascape Inc. ~~Ms. Maxwell played Melinda, the kleptomaniac heiress, in the soap opera Edge of Our Lives.~~

UNCOMBINED

Leslie Morris will be the guest speaker at next week's Friends of Maligned Felines dinner. She owns 14 cats and has written extensively about the creative uses of kitty litter.

COMBINED

Leslie Morris, **who owns 14 cats and has written extensively about the creative use of kitty litter,** will be the guest speaker at next week's Friends of Maligned Felines dinner. ~~She owns 14 cats and has written extensively about the decorative uses of kitty litter.~~

Or:

~~Leslie Morris will be~~ **The guest speaker at next week's Friends of Maligned Felines dinner will**

be Leslie Morris, ~~She~~ **who** owns 14 cats and has written extensively about the creative uses of kitty litter.

UNCOMBINED
Murphy has hired B. Breaker and Associates. It is a law firm well known for its hardball tactics.

COMBINED
Murphy has hired B. Breaker and Associates, ~~It is~~ a law firm well known for its hardball tactics.

UNCOMBINED
Harry Highstepper scored 43 points last night to spark the Beluga Warriors to a 98–93 victory over the Transylvania Knights. Highstepper had been averaging only 10 points a game throughout the season.

COMBINED
Harry Highstepper, **who had been averaging only 10 points a game throughout the season**, scored 43 points last night to spark the Beluga Warriors to a 98–93 victory over the Transylvania Knights. ~~Highstepper had been averaging only 11 points a game throughout the season.~~

SUBORDINATE AFTERTHOUGHTS

Yet another useful and familiar combining pattern is to add a subordinate clause or, more commonly, a phrase or series of phrases to the *back* end of a sentence. The main advantage of "backloading" sentences in this way is that the main thought of the sentence has already been established in the reader's mind, which means that the reader has already created an umbrella for that information. You need to make sure, of course, that the combined element connects logically to the idea that immediately precedes it. Otherwise, you end up with a dangling modifier.

Here are several examples that illustrate the pattern. Notice that in each instance, the combined elements are closely related. Notice, too, that you can use different structures—a phrase or a clause—as the vehicle for the imported element.

UNCOMBINED
Had Eleanor chosen to, she could have assumed all the responsibility herself. She could have left her sister with nothing to do but look after the ant farm.

COMBINED
Had Eleanor chosen to, she could have assumed all the responsibility herself, ~~She could have left~~ **leaving** her sister with nothing to do but look after the ant farm.

Or:

Had Eleanor chosen to, she could have assumed all the responsibility herself, ~~She could have left~~ **which would have left** her sister with nothing to do but look after the ant farm.

Or:

Had Eleanor chosen to, she could have assumed all the responsibility herself, ~~She could have left~~ **a situation that would have left** her sister with nothing to do but look after the ant farm.

UNCOMBINED
The two principals in this dispute have refused to speak to one another. They have chosen instead to communicate through their lawyers.

COMBINED
The two principals in this dispute have refused to speak to one another, ~~They have chosen,~~ **choosing** instead to communicate through their lawyers.

Or:

The two principals in this dispute have refused to speak to one another, ~~They have chosen~~ **their communication taking place** ~~to communicate~~ through their lawyers.

UNCOMBINED
After his third glass of wine Chadwick began to relax. His voice softened. His smile returned.

COMBINED
After his third glass of wine Chadwick began to relax, his voice ~~softened.~~ **softening,** his smile ~~returned~~ **returning.**

UNCOMBINED
The issue here comes down to morality. It's a simple matter of right or wrong.

COMBINED
The issue here comes down to morality ~~It's~~ —a simple matter of right or wrong.

As these examples amply illustrate, it doesn't make that much difference whether the tacked-on element has been expressed as a clause or as a phrase introduced by a gerund.

That choice is usually a matter of preference, although it's wise to vary the pattern. In the following example, you will see how humorist Dave Barry uses "add-on" subordinate phrases to play off the content of the main clause. Note, too, that every sentence in this paragraph ends with a subordinate clause that *could* have operated as a sentence unto itself—but not with the same impact.

If you're like most people, as you enter your forties you start to become farsighted, **which simply means that you won't be able to read any document located within your immediate Zip Code.** The solution is to wear "bifocals," **which are a special kind of eyeglasses that somehow make the world look different but not any clearer.** The best angle for looking through bifocals is when you lean way back and look through the lens bottoms, **thus affording the public a spectacular panoramic view of your nasal passages**; although a lot of people also get results by wearing their bifocals up on their foreheads, **thus allowing the light rays to bypass the eyeballs altogether and penetrate the brain directly.**

INSIDE MOVES

The most difficult challenge in combining is to integrate a *series* of modifying elements into the interior of a sentence. You need to be careful of two things. One is clarity—making sure your readers will have no problem connecting the modifying element to the idea it's meant to modify. The other is rhythm—making sure that when the imported element sets up shop in the "host" sentence, it meshes well with the elements that are already there.

The following examples of professional writing—the first from Mary-Lou Weisman and the second fr om Mark Helprin—will give you a chance to observe how writers with a wonderful ear for sentence rhythms use this technique. The first paragraph in each set replicates the way the paragraph was originally written. The second is a doctored version in which the combined elements now sit in their own sentences. And the third paragraph gives you a closer look of how each of these writers has has woven the sentence. What is important to keep in mind as you read through these sentences is that the interior elements of the sentence add texture and interest, but do not corrupt the clarity of the sentence and do not create an awkward rhythm.

MARY-LOU WEISMAN

Whenever two or more married couples gather together to socialize, it's not just a party, it's a masquerade. One upmanship becomes a duet, as both husband and wife conspire, he behind his mask, she behind hers, to present in the best possible light the third persona they have brought to the party: their marriage.

DOCTORED VERSION (NO COMBINING)

Whenever two or more married couples gather together to socialize, it's not just a party, it's a masquerade. One upmanship becomes a duet. Both husband and wife conspire to present in the best possible light the third persona they have brought to the party. The persona is their marriage. He is behind his mask. She is behind hers.

An Inside Look

Whenever two or more married couples gather together to socialize, it's not just a party, it's a masquerade. One upmanship becomes a duet, **as both husband and wife conspire, he behind his mask, she behind hers,** ~~Both husband and wife conspire~~ to present in the best possible light the third persona they have brought to the party: **their marriage.** ~~The persona is their marriage. He is behind his masks. She is behind hers.~~

Mark Helprin

The letters you receive are in ecru and blue envelopes, with crests, stamps reminiscent of the Italian miniaturists, and, sometimes, varicolored wax seals over ribbon. Even before you read them the sight of the penmanship gives away their authors and may be the cause for comfort, dread, amusement, curiosity or disgust. And, as you read, following the idiomatic, expressive, and imprecise swells and dips like a sailor in a small boat on an agitated sea, the hand of your correspondent reinforces his thoughts, as do the caesuras rhythmically arrayed in conjunction with the need to dip the pen.

Doctored Version (Uncombined)

The letters you receive are in ecru and blue envelopes. The crest and stamps are reminiscent of the Italian miniaturists. Sometimes they are reminiscent of varicolored wax seals over ribbon. Even before you read them, the sight of the penmanship gives away their authors. This sight may be the cause for comfort, dread, amusement, curiosity or disgust. And, as you read, you follow the idiomatic, expressive, and imprecise swells and dips. You are like a sailor in a small boat on an agitated sea. The hand of your correspondent reinforces his thought. The caesuras are rhythmically arrayed in conjunction with the need to dip the pen.

AN INSIDE LOOK
The letters you receive are in ecru and blue envelopes, ~~They have~~ **with** crests and stamps. ~~The crests and stamps are~~ reminiscent of the Italian miniaturists, **and,** ~~sometimes there are~~ varicolored wax seals over ribbon. Even before you read them, the sight of the penmanship gives away their authors ~~This sight~~ **and** may be the cause for comfort, dread, amusement, curiosity or disgust. **And,** as you read,- ~~you follow~~ following the idiomatic, expressive, and imprecise swells and dips like a sailor in a small boat on an agitated sea, the hand of your correspondent reinforces his thoughts, as do the caesuras rhythmically arrayed in conjunction with the need to dip the pen.

THE PERILS OF OVER-COMBINING

Regardless of how skillfully you integrate subordinate elements into your sentences, you can't push the envelope too far. Readers have a limit to how many levels of subordination and parenthetical information they can handle in the same sentence. To experience that limit for yourself, read the following sentence:

Few Philadelphians who know Ms. Adams, whose confrontational style has made her popular with her mostly conservative listeners even though she is a

radical feminist, doubt her when she vows to fight
what she perceives as an effort to silence her.

This sentence has plenty of problems, but the problems have
little to do with either the sequence of clauses or with the number
of words that separate the subject of the sentence "Philadelphians,"
from its verb "doubt." The problem with the sentence is that it is
over-combined. You get so bogged down with the whole business
of Ms. Adams being popular with her conservative listeners, even
though she is a radical feminist, that by the time you get to the verb,
"doubt," you've lost track of the the main idea of the sentence—that
Ms. Adams is a woman of her word.

If you were to parse this sentence, you would *see* these multiple
levels of subordination.

> Few Philadelphians [subject]
>> who know Ms. Adams as a fiercely single-
>> minded woman [subordinated level #1]
>>> whose confrontational style has made
>>> her popular with her mostly conservative
>>> listeners [subordinated level #2]
>>>> even though she is a radical
>>>> feminist [sub. clause #3]
> doubt her [verb and complement]
>> when she vows to fight what she perceives as
>> an effort to silence her.

Creating order

Therapy for over-combined sentences is straightforward. One
way or the other, you need to *reduce* the levels of subordination. You
can do this in one of two ways: You can convert the subordinate into

independent clauses or separate sentences; you can make some of the elements parenthetical instead of subordinate.

Independent thinking. This is the simplest way to edit over-combined and over-subordinated sentences. You simply create separate sentences, with the key ideas occupying the independent clauses of each sentence. Your writing may lose some texture if you "declausify" your sentences in this way, but the writing will usually read more clearly.

> ~~Few Philadelphians who know~~ Ms. Adams ~~as~~ **is** a fiercely single-minded woman, whose confrontational style has made her popular with her mostly conservative listeners, even though she is a radical feminist. **Yet,** few Philadelphians who know her doubt her when she vows to fight what she perceives as an effort to silence her.

If you look again at the edited version of this sentence, you will see that the first of the two sentences still contains two subordinate elements—"whose confrontational style...," and "even though...." The difference between this sentence and the original, however, is that the first of the two examples below begins with an independent clause—Ms. Adams is a fiercely single-minded woman."

Making elements parenthetical. With this approach, the number of subordinate elements in the sentence stays the same. You simply change how they relate to one another. Instead of being subordinate to one another, the subordinated elements become either coordinate—of equal importance—or parenthetical. Here's a look at how the technique can work in a typically over-combined sentence.

> To get an idea of where, among the world's Web sites, which are increasing by many thousands throughout the week, the information you want might be, you rely on specialized search programs

like Yahoo and Webcrawler, which attempt to keep
a current master list of Web sites.

The problem with this sentence lies with that long—and fairly
important—clause that begins with "which" and ends with "week."
This clause is subordinate to a phrase ("among the world's Web
sites") that is, in turn, subordinate to the introductory phrase ("to
get an idea of where"). To make matters worse, you have to work
hard to identify the subject and its verb.

You could probably remedy this problem by rewriting the
sentence. Better therapy, though, would be to take that long phrase
and enclose it in parentheses:

> To get an idea of where, among the world's Web
> sites the information you want might be (and Web
> sites, by the way, are increasing by many thousands
> throughout the week), you rely on specialized
> search programs like Yahoo and Webcrawler, which
> attempt to keep a current master list of Web sites.

Let me make a brief speech about parenthetical expressions.
They can be useful devices, but you need to make sure that the
positing of the parenthetical expression doesn't interfere with the
reader's ability to stay connected to the train of thought. Notice how
much more awkward the sentence you've just read becomes when the
parenthetical phrase gets inserted where it *doesn't* belong.

> To get an idea of where, among the world's Web sites
> (and Web sites, by the way, are increasing by many
> thousands throughout the week) the information
> you want might be, you rely on specialized search
> programs like Yahoo and Webcrawler, which
> attempt to keep a current master list of Web sites.

Your ear should tell you that such a break is awkward. If it doesn't tell you this, then you probably shouldn't be messing around with parenthetical phrases. Rely instead on the first of the first option. It tends to be more "ear" proof.

Printed in the United States
by Baker & Taylor Publisher Services